The Educator's Cookbook 🔍

Google Apps™
Classroom

Authors

Kyle Brumbaugh, M.A.Admin.

Elizabeth Calhoon, M.S.Ed.

Ramsey Musallam, Ed.D.

Robert Pronovost, M.A.Ed.

Catlin Tucker, M.A.Ed.

SHELL EDUCATION

Google Trademark Notices

Google and the Google logo are registered trademarks of Google Inc., used with permission.
© 2012 Google Inc. All rights reserved. Google Apps is a trademark of Google Inc.

Standards

Standards•S © 2007 International Society for Technology in Education (ISTE/NETS)
© 2007 Teachers of English to Speakers of Other Languages, Inc. (TESOL)
© 2007 Board of Regents of the University of Wisconsin System. World-Class Instructional Design and Assessment (WIDA).
© Copyright 2010. National Governors Association Center for Best Practices and Council of Chief State School Officers. All rights reserved.

Shell Education

5301 Oceanus Drive
Huntington Beach, CA 92649-1030
http://www.shelleducation.com
ISBN 978-1-4258-1312-3
© 2014 Shell Educational Publishing, Inc.

Table of Contents

About This Cookbook

Just as anyone can cook, anyone can use Google. When we get our start in the kitchen, it is imperative to have recipes and cookbooks to guide our way. As we become more confident in our cooking skills and learn the difference between a chop and a julienne (some of us are still trying to figure that one out), we venture out, try new things, and ultimately build our own recipe boxes.

The purpose of this "cookbook" is to give both the beginner and the seasoned Google-using teacher some recipes to use and share in the classroom. This cookbook should be as used and as well-loved as your favorite cookbook—you know, the one that you go to every time you need inspiration because it is chock-full of your favorites. When someone asks you for a recipe, you use "that cookbook." This Google cookbook is "that cookbook" for teaching with Google Apps in the classroom. And, as with any cookbook, there are some basic navigation helpers provided along the way. For information on how to navigate through each lesson, see pages 5–8. **Note:** You must sign up for a Google account in order to access the apps presented in this book.

Each recipe is categorized based on whether it is an appetizer, an entrée, a side dish, or a dessert. The entire cookbook is organized based on the type of dish you are looking for. See below for descriptions of each type of dish.

Appetizers can be used as class or unit warm-ups. The **Appetizer Recipes** take relatively little time to prepare and execute.

Entrées are the centerpieces of meals. Use the **Entrée Recipes** when you want a fresh take on an old standby lesson or recipe you have used before.

Side dishes are those dishes we all love to sign up for at potlucks. They can be added to any entrée. You can use the **Side Dish Recipes** at any point in your lesson or unit.

Desserts are the decadent, fun, sweet part of every meal. The **Dessert Recipes** are lively, creative lessons to enjoy in your classroom.

In the appendix, you will find **Preparations**, which are step-by-step instructions for using a variety of Google applications. Review these detailed instructions before starting a recipe. (Each recipe tells you which Preparations are relevant to that lesson.)

Share Your Experiences!

Enjoy diving in and dishing out these recipes. Contact any of the authors about your own recipes or ways you have used them. We love pictures!

elizabeth.calhoon@gmail.com
brumbaugh@gmail.com
ramsey.musallam@gmail.com
catlinrtucker@gmail.com
robert.pronovost@gmail.com

How to Use This Book

Each recipe has elements that focus your use of the Google application(s) for real, practical use in the classroom. The following information will help you execute each recipe.

The **Teacher Technology Skill Level** is based on your own professional self-assessment. If you think you are a technology newbie, try the beginner recipes. For more information on this, see page 7.

The **Student Difficulty Level** indicates the level that is most appropriate for students, but if you find that the recipe can be tweaked for another level, get creative and add your own spices so it works for you! For more information on this, see page 7.

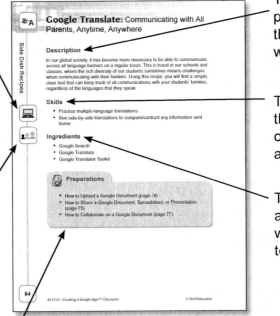

The **Description** provides an overview of the recipe and what you will be doing.

The **Skills** describe the student learning outcome(s) that will be achieved.

The **Ingredients** list all of the materials or websites you will need to complete the recipe.

The **Preparations** provide a quick look at the Google application(s) that are needed before you begin each lesson. For more information on this, see page 6.

How to Use This Book *(cont.)*

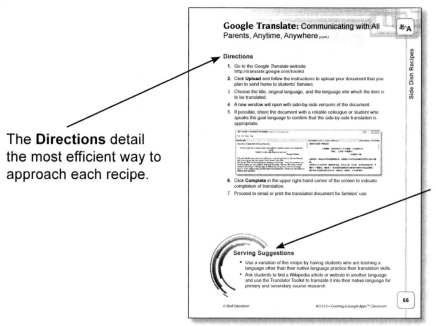

The **Directions** detail the most efficient way to approach each recipe.

The **Serving Suggestions** indicate options for projects in different academic disciplines, variations that can make preparation easier, or how to integrate multiple recipes.

Preparations Overview

Many recipes require a chef to learn specific preparations before the cooking begins. Be sure to review the **Preparations** in this book prior to implementing each recipe. They will provide step-by-step directions on how to use specific Google applications. The preparations are available in the appendix (pages 67–125).

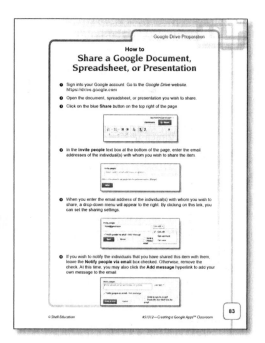

How to Use This Book *(cont.)*

Using the Icons

Level of Difficulty Icons

The level of difficulty icons throughout this book provide quick and easy ways to identify the technology comfort level that is needed to implement the lessons. Review the descriptions below to understand what each icon means.

Teacher Technology Skill Level

 If one level is shaded, the recipe is intended for beginning technology users and above.

 If two levels are shaded, the recipe is intended for intermediate technology users and above.

 If three levels are shaded, the recipe is intended for advanced technology users.

Student Difficulty Level

 If one person is shaded, the recipe is intended for all students, beginning as young as first or second grade.

 If two people are shaded, the recipe is intended for students in fourth grade and above.

 If three people are shaded, the recipe is intended for students in seventh grade and above.

#51312—*Creating a Google Apps™ Classroom*

How to Use This Book *(cont.)*

Using the Icons *(cont.)*

Google App Icons

Before starting each lesson, look at the top corner of the page to see which Google app you will be using. Review the icons and names of the apps before beginning the lessons.

Google Maps

Google Docs

Google Scripts

Blogger

Google Calendar and Gmail

YouTube and Google+ Hangouts

Google Drive

Google Search and Drive

Google Sites

Google Plus

Google Forms

Google Voice

Google Alerts and Scholar

Google Translate

YouTube and Goo.gl

Google Drawings

Google Presentations

Correlation to the Standards

Shell Education is committed to producing educational materials that are research and standards based. As part of this effort, we have correlated all of our products to the academic standards of all 50 states, the District of Columbia, the Department of Defense Dependents Schools, and all Canadian provinces.

How to Find Standards Correlations

To print a customized correlation report of this product for your state, visit our website at **http://www.shelleducation.com** and follow the on-screen directions. If you require assistance in printing correlation reports, please contact our Customer Service Department at 1-877-777-3450.

Purpose and Intent of Standards

Legislation mandates that all states adopt academic standards that identify the skills students will learn in kindergarten through grade twelve. Many states also have standards for Pre–K. This same legislation sets requirements to ensure the standards are detailed and comprehensive.

Standards are designed to focus instruction and guide adoption of curricula. Standards are statements that describe the criteria necessary for students to meet specific academic goals. They define the knowledge, skills, and content students should acquire at each level. Standards are also used to develop standardized tests to evaluate students' academic progress. Teachers are required to demonstrate how their lessons meet state standards. State standards are used in the development of all of our products, so educators can be assured they meet the academic requirements of each state.

International Society for Technology in Education Standards

Many lessons in this book are aligned to the International Society for Technology in Education Standards (ISTE). The standards support the objectives presented throughout the lessons.

Common Core State Standards

Many lessons in this book are aligned to the Common Core State Standards (CCSS). The standards support the objectives presented throughout the lessons.

TESOL and WIDA Standards

The lessons in this book promote English language development for English language learners. The standards support the language objectives presented throughout the lessons.

Correlation to the Standards (cont.)

Standards Chart

Common Core State Standards	Lesson(s)
CCSS.ELA-LITERACY.CCRA.R.1—Read closely to determine what the text says explicitly and to make logical inferences from it; cite specific textual evidence when writing or speaking to support conclusions drawn from the text.	Google Drive: Literature Circles, p. 29; Google Drive: Analyzing Texts, p. 51
CCSS.ELA-LITERACY.CCRA.R.10—Read and comprehend complex literary and informational texts independently and proficiently.	Google Drive: Literature Circles, p. 29
CCSS.ELA-LITERACY.CCRA.R.2—Determine central ideas or themes of a text and analyze their development; summarize the key supporting details and ideas.	Google Drive: Literature Circles, p. 29
CCSS.ELA-LITERACY.CCRA.W.1—Write arguments to support claims in an analysis of substantive topics or texts using valid reasoning and relevant and sufficient evidence.	Google+: Posting Persuasive Reviews, p. 38
CCSS.ELA-LITERACY.CCRA.W.3—Write narratives to develop real or imagined experiences or events using effective technique, well-chosen details and well-structured event sequences.	Google Maps: My Life on a Map, p. 14
CCSS.ELA-LITERACY.CCRA.W.4—Produce clear and coherent writing in which the development, organization, and style are appropriate to task, purpose, and audience.	Google Maps: My Life on a Map, p. 14
CCSS.ELA-LITERACY.CCRA.W.5—Develop and strengthen writing as needed by planning, revising, editing, rewriting, or trying a new approach.	Google Maps: My Life on a Map, p. 14
CCSS.ELA-LITERACY.CCRA.W.6—Use technology, including the Internet, to produce and publish writing and to interact and collaborate with others.	Google Maps: My Life on a Map, p. 14; Google Search and Drive: Expert Group Investigations—Research, Collaborate, and Present, p. 32; Google+: Posting Persuasive Reviews, p. 38; Google Forms and QR Codes: Creating Interactive Anchor Charts, p. 40; Google Drive: Analyzing Texts, p. 51
CCSS.ELA-LITERACY.CCRA.W.7—Conduct short as well as more sustained research projects based on focused questions, demonstrating understanding of the subject under investigation.	Google Search and Drive: Expert Group Investigations—Research, Collaborate, and Present, p. 32; Google Drive: Searching and Evaluating Resource Credibility, p. 48; Google+: Hanging Out with Experts, p. 63
CCSS.ELA-LITERACY.CCRA.W.8—Gather relevant information from multiple print and digital sources, assess the credibility and accuracy of each source, and integrate the information while avoiding plagiarism.	Google Search and Drive: Expert Group Investigations—Research, Collaborate, and Present, p. 32; Google Drive: Searching and Evaluating Resource Credibility, p. 48; Google+: Hanging Out with Experts, p. 63
CCSS.ELA-LITERACY.CCRA.W.9—Draw evidence from literary or informational texts to support analysis, reflection, and research.	Google Drive: Searching and Evaluating Resource Credibility, p. 48
CCSS.ELA-LITERACY.CCRA.SL.1—Prepare for and participate effectively in a range of conversations and collaborations with diverse partners, building on others' ideas and expressing their own clearly and persuasively.	Google Search and Drive: Expert Group Investigations—Research, Collaborate, and Present, p. 32
CCSS.ELA-LITERACY.CCRA.SL.5—Make strategic use of digital media and visual displays of data to express information and enhance understanding of presentations.	YouTube and Google+ Hangouts: Creating Song Parodies, p. 26; Google Search and Drive: Expert Group Investigations—Research, Collaborate, and Present, p. 32; Google Maps: Collaborative Map Making, p. 46; YouTube: Create Your Own Adventure, p. 61

Correlation to the Standards *(cont.)*

Common Core State Standards	Lesson(s)
CCSS.ELA-LITERACY.CCRA.SL.2—Integrate and evaluate information presented in diverse media and formats, including visually, quantitatively, and orally.	Google Search and Drive: Expert Group Investigations—Research, Collaborate, and Present, p. 32
CCSS.ELA-LITERACY.CCRA.SL.4—Present information, findings, and supporting evidence such that listeners can follow the line of reasoning and the organization, development, and style are appropriate to task, purpose, and audience.	Google Search and Drive: Expert Group Investigations—Research, Collaborate, and Present, p. 32
CCSS.ELA-LITERACY.CCRA.L.1—Demonstrate command of the conventions of standard English grammar and usage when writing or speaking.	Google Maps: My Life on a Map, p. 14
CCSS.ELA-LITERACY.CCRA.L.2—Demonstrate command of the conventions of standard English capitalization, punctuation, and spelling when writing.	Google Maps: My Life on a Map, p. 14
CCSS.ELA-LITERACY.CCRA.L.5—Demonstrate understanding of figurative language, word relationships, and nuances in word meanings.	Google Maps: My Life on a Map, p. 14
CCSS.ELA-LITERACY.RH.9-10.3—Analyze in detail a series of events described in a text; determine whether earlier events caused later ones or simply preceded them.	Google Maps: Collaborative Map Making, p. 46
CCSS.ELA-LITERACY.WHST.6—Use technology, including the Internet, to produce and publish writing and present the relationships between information and ideas clearly and efficiently.	Google Maps: Collaborative Map Making, p. 46
CCSS.ELA-LITERACY.WHST.7—Conduct short research projects to answer a question (including a self-generated question), drawing on several sources and generating additional related, focused questions that allow for multiple avenues of exploration.	Google Drive: Searching and Evaluating Resource Credibility, p. 48; Google Alerts and Scholar: Easy Research, p. 52
CCSS.ELA-LITERACY.WHST.8—Gather relevant information from multiple print and digital sources, using search terms effectively; assess the credibility and accuracy of each source; and quote or paraphrase the data and conclusions of others while avoiding plagiarism and following a standard format for citation.	Google Drive: Searching and Evaluating Resource Credibility, p. 48; Google Alerts and Scholar: Easy Research, p. 52
CCSS.ELA-LITERACY.WHST.9—Draw evidence from informational texts to support analysis reflection, and research.	Google Drive: Searching and Evaluating Resource Credibility, p. 48

#51312—*Creating a Google Apps™ Classroom*

Correlation to the Standards (cont.)

International Society for Technology in Education Standards	Lesson(s)
1.Creativity and Innovation—Students demonstrate creative thinking, construct knowledge, and develop innovative products and processes using technology.	Blogger: Class Discussions Made Easy, p. 21; YouTube and Google+ Hangouts: Creating Song Parodies, p. 26; Google Drive: Literature Circles, p. 29; Google Search and Drive: Expert Group Investigations—Research, Collaborate, and Present, p. 32; Google Sites and Other Google Tools: Bringing Everything Together, p. 35; Coding in Google Sites: Getting Geeky, p. 43; Google Maps: Collaborative Map Making, p. 46; YouTube: Create Your Own Adventure, p. 61
1a.Creativity and Innovation—Students apply existing knowledge to generate new ideas, products, or processes.	Google Drawings: Interactive Concept Maps, p. 58
1b.Creativity and Innovation—Students create original works as a means of personal or group expression.	Google Drawings: Interactive Concept Maps, p. 58; Google Presentations: Quickly Digitize Student Work, p. 65
1c.Creativity and Innovation—Students use models and simulations to explore complex systems and issues.	Google Drawings: Interactive Concept Maps, p. 58
1d.Creativity and Innovation—Students identify trends and forecast possibilities.	Google Drawings: Interactive Concept Maps, p. 58
2.Communication and Collaboration—Students use digital media and environments to communicate and work collaboratively, including at a distance, to support individual learning and contribute to the learning of others.	Google Docs: Class Drop/Pick-Up Box, p. 16; Blogger: Class Discussions Made Easy, p. 21; Google Calendar and Gmail: Class Reminders, p. 23; Google Drive: Literature Circles, p. 29; Google Search and Drive: Expert Group Investigations—Research, Collaborate, and Present, p. 32; Google Sites and Other Google Tools: Bringing Everything Together, p. 35; Google Forms and QR Codes: Creating Interactive Anchor Charts, p. 40; Google Voice and Mobile Phones: Silent Brainstorming or Voting, p. 42; Coding in Google Sites: Getting Geeky, p. 43; Google Maps: Collaborative Map Making, p. 46; Google Drive: Analyzing Texts, p. 51; Google Translate: Communicating with All Parents, Anytime, Anywhere, p. 54
2a.Communication and Collaboration—Students interact, collaborate, and publish with peers, experts, or others employing a variety of digital environments and media.	Google Drawings: Interactive Concept Maps, p. 58
2b.Communication and Collaboration—Students communicate information and ideas effectively to multiple audiences.	Google Drawings: Interactive Concept Maps, p. 58; Google Presentations: Quickly Digitize Student Work, p. 65
2d.Communication and Collaboration—Students contribute to project teams to produce original works or solve problems.	Google Forms: Create a Review Game Buzzer, p. 60
3.Research and Information Fluency—Students apply digital tools to gather, evaluate, and use information.	Google Docs: Class Drop/Pick-Up Box, p. 16; Blogger: Class Discussions Made Easy, p. 21; Google Drive: Literature Circles, p. 29; Google Search and Drive: Expert Group Investigations—Research, Collaborate, and Present, p. 32; Google Sites and Other Google Tools: Bringing Everything Together, p. 35; Coding in Google Sites: Getting Geeky, p. 43; Google Maps: Collaborative Map Making, p. 46; Google Drive: Searching and Evaluating Resource Credibility, p. 48; Google Alerts and Scholar: Easy Research, p. 52; Google Translate: Communicating with All Parents, Anytime, Anywhere, p. 54; Google+: Hanging Out with Experts, p. 63
3c.Research and Information—Students evaluate and select information sources and digital tools based on the appropriateness to specific tasks.	YouTube and Goo.gl: Multimedia QR Code Scaffolds, p. 56

Correlation to the Standards *(cont.)*

International Society for Technology in Education Standards	Lesson(s)
3d. Research and Information Fluency—Students process data and report results.	Google Scripts: Grading and Feedback, p. 18
4. Critical Thinking, Problem Solving, and Decision Making—Students use critical thinking skills to plan and conduct research, manage projects, solve problems, and make informed decisions.	Google Docs: Class Drop/Pick-Up Box, p. 16; Blogger: Class Discussions Made Easy, p. 21; Google Drive: Literature Circles, p. 29; Google Search and Drive: Expert Group Investigations—Research, Collaborate, and Present, p. 32; Google Sites and Other Google Tools: Bringing Everything Together, p. 35; Coding in Google Sites: Getting Geeky, p. 43; Google Maps: Collaborative Map Making, p. 46; Google Drive: Searching and Evaluating Resource Credibility, p. 48; Google Alerts and Scholar: Easy Research, p. 52; YouTube: Create Your Own Adventure, p. 61; Google+: Hanging Out with Experts, p. 63
4d. Critical Thinking, Problem Solving, and Decision Making—Students use multiple processes and diverse perspectives to explore alternative solutions.	YouTube and Goo.gl: Multimedia QR Code Scaffolds, p. 56
5. Digital Citizenship—Students understand human, cultural, and societal issues related to technology and practice legal and ethical behavior.	Google Docs: Class Drop/Pick-Up Box, p. 16; Blogger: Class Discussions Made Easy, p. 21; Google Calendar and Gmail: Class Reminders, p. 23; Google Search and Drive: Expert Group Investigations—Research, Collaborate, and Present, p. 32; Google Sites and Other Google Tools: Bringing Everything Together, p. 35; Coding in Google Sites: Getting Geeky, p. 43; Google Drive: Analyzing Texts, p. 51
5b. Digital Citizenship—Students exhibit a positive attitude toward using technology that supports collaboration, learning, and productivity.	Google Scripts: Grading and Feedback, p. 18
6. Technology Operations and Concepts—Students demonstrate a sound understanding of technology concepts, systems, and operations.	Google Docs: Class Drop/Pick-Up Box, p. 16; Blogger: Class Discussions Made Easy, p. 21; Google Calendar and Gmail: Class Reminders, p. 23; Google Search and Drive: Expert Group Investigations—Research, Collaborate, and Present, p. 32; Google Sites and Other Google Tools: Bringing Everything Together, p. 35; Coding in Google Sites: Getting Geeky, p. 43
6a. Technology Operations and Concepts—Students understand and use technology systems.	All Lessons
6b. Technology Operations and Concepts—Students select and use applications effectively and productively.	Google Scripts: Grading and Feedback, p. 18

TESOL and WIDA Standards	Lesson(s)
English language learners communicate for social, intercultural, and instructional purposes within a school setting.	All Lessons
English language learners communicate information, ideas, and concepts necessary for academic success in the area of language arts.	All Lessons

Google Maps: My Life on a Map

Description

A blank page can be daunting for any writer, especially young writers who are unsure of their abilities. Teach narrative writing slowly and use maps combined with media to get students thinking about their lives and their stories before they put pen to paper (or type their work). Once students have created maps detailing major events in their lives, they will feel more confident writing narrative pieces.

Skills

- Create a map using Google Maps.
- Add pins, text, and pictures to individual maps.
- Identify major events in one's life and describe their significance.

Ingredients

- personal digital pictures (*optional*)
- Google Maps

Preparations

- How to Create a Google Map (page 96)
- How to Add Collaborators to a Google Map (page 97)
- How to Share a Google Map (page 98)
- How to Add Pins to a Google Map (page 99)
- How to Add Text to a Google Map (page 100)
- How to Change Pins in a Google Map (page 101)
- How to Embed Multimedia Content into a Google Map (page 103)
- How to Draw Lines Between Locations in a Google Map (page 104)

Directions

1. Log into your Google account.
2. Navigate to the *Google Maps* website.
   http://maps.google.com
3. Go to the gear menu and click **My Places**.
4. Click **Create New Map**.

5. Add collaborators. Remember that the teacher should always be added as a collaborator. Teachers who use writing groups to support students in the various stages of their writing should remind students to add the other members of their writing groups as collaborators. This way the members of the group can provide feedback to each other in these early stages of the writing process.

6. Give the map a title and description. Ask students to title their maps "[First and Last Name's] Life on a Map."

7. Make this life map unlisted. This can be changed later, but we suggest unlisted to start.

8. Click **Save**.

9. Enter an address in the search box for each life event that will need to be saved to the map. Click **Save to Map** and save all the locations to the map that was just created. Teachers should decide on the number of events students need to create on their maps in preparation for their narratives.

10. When all locations are entered in the map, return to My Places and click on your map.

11. Add pins, pictures, and text. Lines can also be added. These tools are located at the top of the map.

12. For each pin, label the event with the following information: date, brief description of the event, people present, sensory details and emotions associated with the event.

13. Click on each individual location on the map to add text, embed pictures, and draw lines marking the chronology of events from the first to the last event.

14. When students have completed their maps, ask them to use their maps as a reference as they write their narratives.

Serving Suggestions

- Create a life map for narrative writing.
- Chronicle the events of another person's life.
- Map individual events for an important historical time period.
- Chart the individual events for a fictional event, character, or story.

Google Docs: Class Drop/Pick-Up Box

Description

One of the toughest things for teachers to manage in our digital world is the number of digital documents that students will produce and then submit to their teachers. This recipe provides a way to create a drop box that all students can access. They can then submit their work to this drop box. Teachers can also reverse the process to create a pick-up box for your students to get activity sheets or other handouts.

Skills

- Learn how to turn in assignments in a digital format.
- Help teachers and students manage digital content.

Ingredients

- Google Drive
- Google Forms

Preparations

- How to Create a Google Form (page 75)
- How to Create a Google Folder (page 86)
- How to Share a Google Folder (page 87)

Directions

1. In your Google Drive account, create a folder/collection for each class. In an elementary setting, you would have only one box.

2. When naming this folder/collection, make sure that you give it a title that will easily identify it for your students.

3. Collect the Google Drive usernames for all students. The best way to do this would be to use a Google Form where students provide their user names. If you have Google Apps™ for Education, the form can collect the username information for you. You may want to have this as part of your start of the year collection of information from students. If you are going to use this with parents, you will want them to fill out separate forms.

4. In the Sharing settings for this folder, set the folder to be shared with the students by copying and pasting the list of students' Google accounts. For the drop box, you will need to set the sharing settings to Can Edit. For the pick-up box, choose **Can View** in the Sharing settings dialogue box.

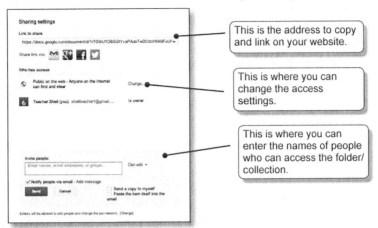

5. From the Sharing settings dialogue box, copy the link for the box and post it on your website, or send the link to others through email.

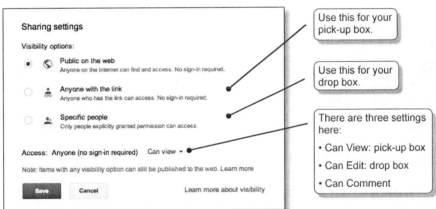

6. You can test the process by having students place informational documents in the folder/collection. By repeating this process, you can create multiple boxes for your classes.

Serving Suggestions

- Students can build their own ePortfolios to share with parents.
- Provide copies of school/district forms so that parents have easy access to them.

Google Scripts: Grading and Feedback

Description

In today's high-stakes testing environment, a myriad of options exists for quickly grading and analyzing student performance on multiple-choice-type items. Despite such analysis, providing students with rapid, formative feedback upon conclusion of an assessment is not a common automated feature. To address this need, teachers can insert a Google Script (a code that creates automated tasks) into a Google Form template to gather student exam responses, automatically grade and analyze the items, and provide targeted, customized feedback to each student via email. The sooner students receive their feedback, the sooner they can be successful in future attempts.

Skills

- Access and use a Google form to record item responses.
- Gather automated feedback to incorrect responses via email.
- Reflect on incorrect responses.

Ingredients

- Google Drive
- Google Forms
- Google Spreadsheets

Preparations

- How to Create a Google Form (page 75)
- How to Add Questions to a Google Form (page 76)
- How to Copy a Link to a Google Form (page 78)
- How to Insert a Script into a Google Spreadsheet (page 80)

Directions

1. Create a multiple-choice assessment, either on paper or on a Google form, that assesses student knowledge on a particular topic.
2. Log into your Google account and navigate to the *Google Drive* website. **https://drive.google.com**
3. Click on **Create** and **Form** to create a new Google form.
4. Title your form according to the assessment topic.

5. Add your questions. If using a paper test, simply add an item response template for students to fill in accordingly (i.e., 1. A, B, C, D, E; 2. A, B, C, D, E).

6. Click **Done** after completing each question.

7. Click on **Choose Response Destination** and select **New Spreadsheet** from the pop-up window, and give the spreadsheet a title.

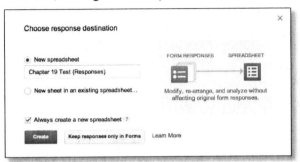

8. Click on **Create**.

9. Click on **View Responses** from the form view to open the spreadsheet.

10. From the spreadsheet view, click on **Tools** and select **Script Gallery** from the drop-down menu.

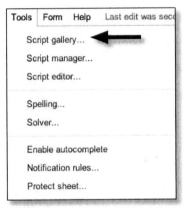

11. Follow script instructions. The content on the **Help page** provides an overview and assistance.

Google Scripts: Grading and Feedback *(cont.)*

12. Click on the **Form** menu and select **Go to live form** and copy the URL from the address bar.

13. To send the form to students or embed the Google form in a blog or website, click on **Edit this form** to navigate back to the original form.

14. From the form view, click on **Send Form**. A new box will appear to allow you to send the form via email, or you can click **Embed** to obtain the code to embed the form in a blog or a website.

15. Deliver the Google form to students prior to, or upon conclusion of, the assessment.

16. Instruct students to record answers on the associated Google form using an appropriate device.

17. Instruct students to access email to view formative exam feedback.

Serving Suggestions

- Use script for short multiple-choice-type warm-up problems in one-to-one environments to promote immediate feedback.
- Replace the Flubaroo script with the MCQ script for more tailored and flexible feedback.

Blogger: Class Discussions Made Easy

Description

Blogger is the original self-publishing tool. It has great built-in features that make it the perfect tool for classes and schools. Blogger provides teachers with as much or as little control as they want and is accessible by more students than any other technology-based tool. Create classroom discussions that continue outside of the classroom and can encompass multiple classes of students, or the world with the power of Blogger. It is the most versatile and accessible of all of the Google tools. It increases access for students and members of a school community, showing them how to collaborate and communicate with ease by breaking down access barriers. **Note:** Be sure to consult copyright laws and fair use before using images or videos in a blog.

Skills

- Write on any topic, and include images, video, or any other Internet-based content.
- Create a blog, and respond to posts by teachers or classmates.

Ingredients

- Blogger
- Any copyright-free, Internet-based images or video

 Preparation

- How to Create a Blogger Page (page 122)

Directions

1. While logged into your Google account, go to the *Blogger* website. **http://www.blogger.com**

2. Set up a new blog by clicking on the **New Blog** link on the left hand side of the page. You will be asked to give your blog a name and a custom Uniform Resource Locator (URL). There are lots of templates and customization options you can use with your blog.

#51312—Creating a Google Apps™ Classroom

Blogger: Class Discussions Made Easy *(cont.)*

3. Once you have created your blog, go to the **Settings** link at the bottom of the menu list and make your choices.

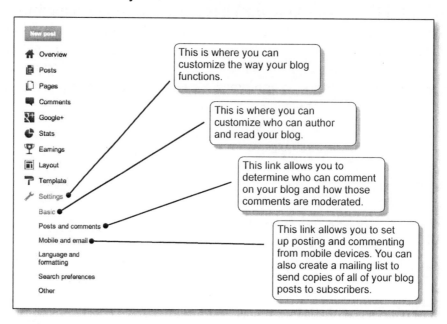

4. Under **Basic**, do the following:
   - Add Authors.
   - Select Viewers.

5. Under **Post** and **Comments**, do the following:
   - Decide who can comment—only authors and viewers or everyone.

6. Under **Mobile** and **Email**, do the following:
   - Set up posting or commenting from a phone or other mobile device.
   - Create a custom email address to send emails to post to your blog.
   - Set up a mailing list that will send an email out every time you or another author posts to your blog.

Serving Suggestions

   - Use this in lieu of a weekly newsletter for elementary teachers.
   - Assign homework where students can ask questions using comments.
   - Hold class discussions and even extend the learning outside class or during a "fish bowl" activity.
   - Using Blogger in conjunction with Google Reader is another way for teachers and other students to see student work without having to collect it every day.

Google Calendar and Gmail:
Class Reminders

Description

Teachers can do so much more than sharing a Google calendar with their students. Google Calendar is a communication tool that can push out reminders to everyone. With the number of communication tools available to teachers and students, this recipe offers a way to cut down on the time wasted in finding just what was assigned. Teachers can send reminders and students can receive them any time, any place!

Skills

- Receive reminders about important class or school activities through a variety of technologies.
- Learn about organization skills and setting deadlines.

Ingredients

- Google calendar
- Gmail
- Google sites
- Blogger
- IFTTT.com
- Twitter

 Preparations

- How to Create a Google Site (page 89)
- How to Embed a Gadget into a Google Site (page 95)
- How to Create a Google Calendar (page 121)
- How to Create a Blogger Page (page 122)
- How to Create Filters in Gmail (page 123)
- How to Add a Gadget on a Blogger Page (page 124)
- How to Create a Recipe in IFTTT (page 125)

Google Calendar and Gmail:
Class Reminders *(cont.)*

Directions

1. Create a new Google calendar to use for these reminders.

   - On the **Share this Calendar** tab, select **Make this calendar public**.

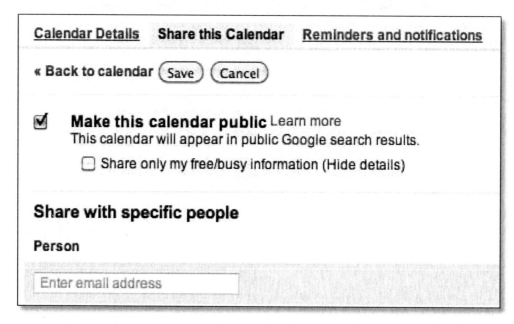

   - On the **Reminders and Notifications** tab select **Add a reminder** and select the number of default reminders you would like to have for each event on your calendar. All of these reminders should be set up as **emails**. A good rule of thumb is to have one reminder a day in advance. You can have up to five reminders for each event.

2. Go to the *If This, Then That (IFTTT)* website.
   https://IFTTT.com

Google Calendar and Gmail:
Class Reminders *(cont.)*

3. Create a new account. IFTTT is a free service that allows you to connect the functions of a variety of web applications together. In this case we will be connecting Gmail and Twitter.

   • Connect your Gmail and Twitter accounts to IFTTT by clicking **Create** at the top of the page. Then, under **Choose Trigger Channel**, select the Gmail icon. Click **Activate**. You must allow IFTTT access to your Gmail account in order to proceed.

   • Next, select **New Email** as the trigger. In the Complete Trigger Fields, add this address: **calendar-notification@google.com** and then click **Create Trigger**.

   • You will then choose an **Action Channel**. Click on the **Twitter** icon. Click **Activate**. You will be prompted to authorize the app. Once you authorize the app, Twitter will be activated.

   • Select **Post a Tweet** then **Create Action** and finally **Create Recipe**.

4. This will create the connection between your Google calendar and Twitter. Have students subscribe to your Twitter account to get updates. You can also embed your Twitter feed into your website by using a tool like **Tweetwally**.

Serving Suggestion

   • Browse other tested recipes that work well with Google Drive. **https://IFTTT.com/recipes?channel=google_drive**

   • Consider having tweets create new lines on a Google spreadsheet—an easy way to keep track of your greatest finds.

   • Try creating a recipe to sync your Dropbox to your Google Drive.

#51312—*Creating a Google Apps™ Classroom*

YouTube and Google+ Hangouts:
Creating Song Parodies

Description

Students are always humming a tune in class. Using this recipe, students may hum a familiar tune, but the words they are singing in their heads will be a reminder of the learning in class. **Note:** You may use self-created song parodies in your classroom as fair use in an educational setting, but consult copyright laws and fair use before sharing them with others. Also, be sure to explain the importance of privacy settings to students. They must be careful when uploading videos to the Internet not to share them publicly.

Skills

* Use prior musical knowledge to engage in a new unit.
* Use big ideas from a unit to create parody lyrics for a popular song.
* Create videos using Google+ Hangouts.

Ingredients

* YouTube
* Google Documents
* Google+
* Google+ Hangouts
* microphone
* computer video camera (*optional*)

 Preparations

* How to Create a Google Document (page 71)
* How to Create a Google Site (page 89)
* How to Embed a YouTube Video into a Google Site (page 93)
* How to Create a YouTube Video (page 105)
* How to Start a Google+ Hangout (page 109)
* How to Broadcast a Google+ Hangout Using Hangouts On Air (page 110)
* How to Share a YouTube Video Within a Google+ Hangout (page 111)

YouTube and Google+ Hangouts:
Creating Song Parodies *(cont.)*

Directions

1. Navigate to the *YouTube* website. **http://www.youtube.com**

2. Search for a song you would like to parody by adding the keyword "karaoke" to the song name.

3. Find the lyrics to the song and modify them to fit to the unit for the class in a Google document. Sometimes, the lyrics are in the karaoke video or description. If not, use Google to search for the lyrics.

4. Start a Google+ Hangout with Hangouts On Air enabled. Unless you are going to sing a duet, you do not need to invite anyone into the Hangout.

5. Name the Hangout the title you would like the YouTube parody video to have when you are finished.

6. Share the YouTube video you wish to sing along to in the Hangout.

7. Before you start playing the video and singing the parody lyrics, click **Start Broadcast** in the upper right-hand corner. This will broadcast your Hangout for others to watch, but they cannot participate.

8. If you are worried about appearing on screen, you can turn off the video by clicking the video camera icon on the tool bar in the top center of the screen. When the icon is red, the camera is off. If the icon is black, the camera is recording.

YouTube and Google+ Hangouts:
Creating Song Parodies *(cont.)*

9. When you are ready, with the parody lyrics out in your Google document, press the **Play** button below the video.

   Note: When you start a video in a Hangout, it mutes your microphone. To override, click on the microphone icon. When the icon is red, the microphone is muted. When the icon is black, the microphone is recording.

   • Do not click the **Push to talk** button, or it will decrease the volume from your video.

   • Do not use headphones. The audio from the karaoke video should be picked up by the microphone. It will not be captured without the microphone on and the volume loud enough for the microphone to pick it up.

10. When you are finished recording your parody song, pause the karaoke video and click **End broadcast**.

11. Your video will be listed and processed shortly after broadcasting. http://www.youtube.com/my_videos

12. Watch the video to ensure the volume of your voice and the background karaoke track are at appropriate volumes.

13. Open this video in class to share the parody or embed the video in your class website or syllabus.

Serving Suggestion

   • Students can create their own videos at the end of a unit to summarize their learning.

#51312—Creating a Google Apps™ Classroom

Google Drive: Literature Circles

Description

Literature circles are a great way to give students of any age choices in reading, thereby increasing their love of reading. Using Google Books, their libraries, and teacher-created templates in Google Drive, literature circles are forever transformed from packets of paper to a completely paperless and more engaging format.

Skills

- Choose an appropriate "outside reading choice" based on reading level.
- Learn to write book reviews.
- Collaborate with other students in Google Drive.

Ingredients

- Google Search
- Google Books
- Google Drive
- Google sites

 ## Preparations

- How to Create a Google Document (page 71)
- How to Collaborate on a Google Document (page 73)
- How to Make a Google Document into a Template (page 74)
- How to Share a Google Document, Spreadsheet, or Presentation (page 83)
- How to Create a Google Site (page 89)
- How to Share and Collaborate on a Google Site (page 90)
- How to Create a Page in Google Sites (page 91)
- How to Embed a Google Document into a Google Site (page 92)
- How to Embed a YouTube Video into a Google Site (page 93)
- How to Create a Google Books Library (page 116)
- How to Create a Google Books Bookshelf (page 117)

#51312—Creating a Google Apps™ Classroom

Google Drive: Literature Circles (cont.)

Directions

1. Search for and add outside reading books to your Google Books library.

2. Once all books are added, create a different shelf for each reading level in your class. You may choose to add a note to each book, to provide guidance to students in their choosing of a book.

3. Share either the entire library, or the specific shelves that you want your students to choose from.

4. Students choose their top three outside reading books. Form groups of four to six students, all of whom will be reading the same book. For older books, there may be the opportunity to read the entire book online or to embed it on a website!

5. Students are then assigned one of the following roles (roles are taken from Jim Burke's *The English Teacher's Companion*): Discussion Director, Illuminator, Illustrator, Connector, Word Watcher, or Summarizer. For specific role definitions in a convenient format, go to Jim Burke's *Lit Circle Roles Bookmark* document. **http://www.englishcompanion. com/pdfDocs/litcirclebookmark. pdf**

6. Create templates in Google Drive modeling the literature circle guides in the literature circle packet linked above.

7. Share the links for the literature circle templates with all students and assign the rotation of students through the roles. (You may choose, instead, to keep one student in a single role for the entire reading of the book.)

8. Provide students with a reading schedule. Allow for at least one full hour once per week for students to work in their literature circle groups.

9. As students complete their readings and group discussions, ask them to embed their completed templates into a Google site, with a separate page for each role. Connectors can use this opportunity to embed YouTube videos or websites. Illustrators could create online drawings or online posters. The possibilities are endless. Consider giving students freedom in their interpretations of their roles.

10. Make sure students share their sites with you from the very beginning of this project.

Serving Suggestions

- Math: Consider asking students to read non-fiction books about mathematical theory or mathematicians.
- Science: Students can be asked to read non-fiction books about scientific theories, both currently or in the past. The Word Watcher role can be particularly useful here, while learning content-specific language.
- Lower grades should be limited to smaller groups, if possible.
- Assessment is most successful if there is shared responsibility. Consider giving both an individual and a group grade for the final product.

Google Search and Drive:
Expert Group Investigations—
Research, Collaborate, and Present

Description

Replace lecturing with this student-driven project that empowers students to become the experts on a topic, then share that knowledge! Students research, discuss information, and collaborate to create a dynamic multimedia presentation to share with the class.

Skills

- Research using Google Search.
- Communicate and collaborate on Google Documents.
- Design a presentation using Google Presentation.
- Practice the presentation with a group using Google+ Hangouts.
- Present on a topic to a group of peers.

Ingredients

- Google Search
- Google+ Hangouts
- Google Presentation
- Google Documents

Preparations

- How to Make a Google Document into a Template (page 74)
- How to Create a Google Presentation (page 81)
- How to Upload a Google Presentation (page 82)
- How to Share a Google Document, Spreadsheet, or Presentation (page 83)
- How to Start a Google+ Hangout (page 109)

Google Search and Drive:
Expert Group Investigations—
Research, Collaborate, and Present *(cont.)*

Directions

1. Select the expert group topics and assign student groups. Small groups of three to four students are recommended.

2. Create a class template for each topic being investigated. This template should have the group's topic as well as directions to guide student work. Ask groups to use the template created for their topic to create their own documents. This document must be shared with all group members and the teacher. Tell students to title their documents **"Expert Group Research: [class period + group's topic]."**

3. Students should begin by brainstorming questions they have about their subject. These questions will guide them during their research. For example, if the topic is "Crime and Punishment in Elizabethan England," they might generate questions like:

   - What were the most common crimes committed during this time period?

   - Were men and women given the same punishment for the same crimes?

   - What instruments of torture were used and why?

4. After students brainstorm questions they want to research, they should determine who will research each subtopic. In the directions included on the template, ask students to identify which group member is researching which questions by putting their names in parentheses next to the questions they plan to research.

5. Groups should use Google Search and/or utilize the research tool inside a shared Google document to explore their topics and become experts. Groups should:

   - Identify important information about their topics.

   - Establish resource credibility and discuss relevance of information.

   - Locate compelling media to complement their presentations.

   - Organize information to be used in their presentations.

6. Individual group members should use Google drawings to create graphs, diagrams, mind maps, and/or artistic elements to be inserted into the Google presentation.

33

Google Search and Drive:
Expert Group Investigations—
Research, Collaborate, and Present (cont.)

7. Once the research phase of the project is complete (approximately two to three days), ask each group to create and share a Google presentation with the title, "Expert Group Presentation: [class period + group's topic]." This Google presentation should be shared with all group members and with the teacher. Each group should use their research and discussions to create a multimedia presentation for the class.

   • Google presentations can be shared with other groups to garner peer feedback prior to the oral presentations.

• Groups should practice their Google presentations using Google+ Hangouts. Each group member should be responsible for particular slides and information.

• Once the Google presentations are complete and groups have had a rehearsal using Google+ Hangouts, have each group present its Google presentation to the class.

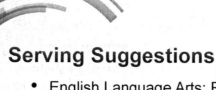

Serving Suggestions

• English Language Arts: Research the historical context of a novel, a collection of authors, literary movements, etc.

• History: Investigate different aspects of a culture, country, or geographic location.

• Science: Explore different types of energy sources, ecosystems, genetic traits, diseases, etc.

• Math: Find out more about different mathematical concepts, important mathematicians, or mathematical mysteries to be solved.

• Foreign Language: Explore influences on the language, different cultural groups speaking that language, holidays/festivities associated with people who speak this language, etc.

Google Sites and Other Google Tools:
Bringing Everything Together

Description

This recipe allows teachers and students to add content from most of the basic Google tools to a Google site. The ability to embed or include this content in the website makes the site more dynamic and encourages visitors (students, parents, etc.) to come back to the site again and again because the content on the site is always updated. Google Sites is also a great tool for collaboration because every page on a Google site has a place for comments at the bottom. (Comments can be moderated or restricted on a page-by-page basis.)

Skills

- Create content using various Google tools.
- Learn to add content easily to a Google site.

Ingredients

- Google Sites
- Google Drive
- Google Calendar
- YouTube
- Google Maps

 Preparations

- How to Create a Google Document (page 71)
- How to Upload a Google Document (page 72)
- How to Share a Google Document, Spreadsheet, or Presentation (page 83)
- How to Create a Google Site (page 89)
- How to Create a Google Map (page 96)
- How to Create a YouTube Video (page 105)
- How to Create a Google Calendar (page 121)

35

Google Sites and Other Google Tools:
Bringing Everything Together *(cont.)*

Directions

1. Once logged into your Google account, navigate to your Google site and click on the **pencil** icon in the upper right corner to open editing mode.

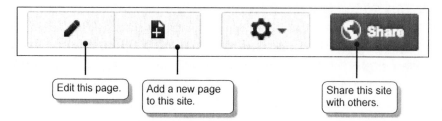

2. Once you have enabled editing mode, a new toolbar will appear, which will allow you to add content to the site.

3. Select **Insert** from the toolbar to reveal the menu shown below.

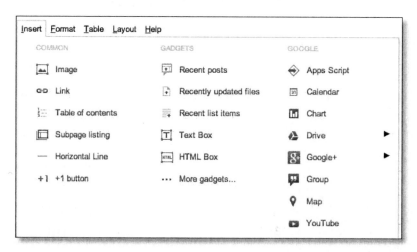

4. Each one of the links will allow you to insert the content listed. The list on the right-hand side of the menu is all of the Google applications/tools that are automatically included when you create your Google account.

- Google Drive: Documents, Spreadsheets, Presentations, Forms, Drawings

- Google Calendar: The Google Sites tool will allow embedding of one Google calendar from the list owned by the user.

- YouTube Video: Will allow the embedding of any publicly accessible YouTube video. This requires the creation of a YouTube account linked to your Google account.

- Google Maps: Will allow the embedding of any publicly accessible Google map.

- Google Groups: Will allow you to embed the public feed of any Google group.

Google Sites and Other Google Tools:
Bringing Everything Together *(cont.)*

Serving Suggestions

- Create a class project website, where each student has a page and the site stands as a collective of all student work. In upper elementary grades, students can publish a site with state profiles, presidential biographies, book reviews, or science projects.

- English: Students can create a book review site, a collaborative poetry site where students can add pictures and prose, or a writer's workshop site where students can read and provide feedback to their classmates.

- Math: Students could create or find images that illustrate the mathematical concepts being taught in class (e.g., students could post a picture of the roof of a house to illustrate the idea of slope). Students could then write about how this concept is applied.

- Science: Create a lab manual site, where every lab in a science class is detailed and reviewed step by step. This could be produced by students collectively to check for understanding and process.

- Social Science: Students can create a thematic website that is a collective of their work. Students in government classes could create pages that document the major findings and historical context of Supreme Court decisions.

- Technical/Vocational Arts: Students could create a collaborative cookbook in culinary arts classes, or a slide show of their work as a personal portfolio.

- If there is content from other Internet-based resources you would like to add to your site, check out the recipe *Coding in Google Sites: Getting Geeky* (pages 43–45). This recipe will allow anyone to add a variety of features into his or her Google site to make the content dynamic.

#51312—*Creating a Google Apps™ Classroom*

Google+: Posting Persuasive Reviews

Description

Every year, students are asked to write reviews or persuasive arguments, yet these persuasive writings are rarely shared beyond the classroom. This recipe will get your students engaged and excited about persuasive writing, as they are asked to publish their writing for others to use in their daily lives.

Skills

- Post a review of a business or place using Google+.
- Write persuasive arguments.

Ingredients

- Google Documents
- Google+

 Preparations

- How to Create a Google Document (page 71)
- How to Share a Google Document, Spreadsheet, or Presentation (page 83)
- How to Post a Local Business Review in Google+ (page 108)

Directions

1. Students should be directed to create a new Google document and share it with their teacher.

2. Ask students to choose a local business such as a restaurant or store and write a review about their experiences with this business. They should focus on being persuasive and concise.

Google+: Posting Persuasive Reviews (cont.)

3. After students have shared their review with their teacher and with fellow students, they should revise and edit the persuasive review.

4. When the review is complete, have students post their reviews on the Google+ Local page for the business.

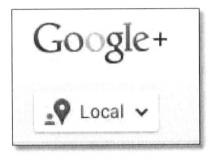

Serving Suggestions

- For those whose students do not have access to Google+ (under age 13 or not supported by the school or district), the teacher can post reviews from his or her own account, with a note such as, "This review is being posted on behalf of one of my second-grade students."
- Persuasive reviews related to a product can also be published on online shopping or consumer review sites.
- Persuasive essays on a topic, not a place or product, can be published to a blog on Blogger.

Google Forms and QR Codes:
Creating Interactive Anchor Charts

Side Dish Recipes

Description

Having students scan the QR code on an anchor chart makes the connection between your previous lessons and students' independent work much stronger. Take pre-existing anchor charts (visuals that document past learning; see example in the directions) and tie them to pre-existing independent work using Google forms and QR codes.

Skill

- Share thoughts, feelings, and reactions through teacher-created Google forms.

Ingredients

- Google Drive and forms
- Goo.gl

Preparations

- How to Create a Google Form (page 75)
- How to Add Questions to a Google Form (page 76)
- How to Shorten a URL Using the Google URL Shortener (page 118)
- How to Resize a QR Code from the Google URL Shortener (page 119)

Directions

1. Think of independent work for students to complete that you would like to tie to an anchor chart. The independent work that goes best with Google Forms is either multiple choice, short-answer questions, or scales (e.g., rate from 1–5).

2. Create a new Google form and title it according to the topic you have chosen. Add the questions you created as independent work.

#51312—Creating a Google Apps™ Classroom

Google Forms and QR Codes:
Creating Interactive Anchor Charts *(cont.)*

3. Copy the URL for the published form from the bottom of the editor.

4. Shorten the URL using the Google URL Shortener (Goo.gl).

5. Resize the QR code to the size you would like.

QR Code

6. Print the QR code and attach it to the anchor chart.

Student Sample

7. Ask students to use a QR code reader to respond to questions during independent work time.

Serving Suggestions

- Replace the Google form with a YouTube video of your lesson related to the anchor chart.
- Replace the Google form with a link to a site with more information on the topic of the anchor chart.
- Replace the Google form with a link to a post on Blogger related to the anchor chart. Have students respond to the post.
- Have students attach QR codes linked to Google form surveys on their research topics to collect data.

Google Voice and Mobile Phones:
Silent Brainstorming or Voting

Side Dish Recipes

Description

Let's go paperless! In this recipe, you will use a Google Voice number to collect student ideas or votes via text messages, without ever sharing your mobile phone number.

Skill

- Share responses via text messages to a teacher's Google Voice number.

Ingredient

- Google Voice

Preparations

- How to Create a Google Voice Number (page 114)

Directions

1. Create a Google Voice number. Choose a number that will be easy for students to remember.

2. Create a simple format for student texts, including a subject tag. This tag can later be used in a search to find all responses to a certain subject. A suggested format is "Student Name, Subject Tag, Response/Vote."

3. Post the Google Voice number and subject tag for students.

4. Pose a question to your class and ask students to text their responses to your Google Voice number in 160 characters or less.

5. Access the student texts through your mobile phone if you have activated text forwarding through the *Google Voice* website. **https://www.google.com/voice#sms**

Serving Suggestion

- Help plan tomorrow's lesson by having students text in questions as they complete work at home.

#51312—Creating a Google Apps™ Classroom

© Shell Education

Coding in Google Sites: Getting Geeky

Description

Teachers often find resources on the Internet that they want to share with their students, but know it might be difficult to guide the students there. Students can create content using a variety of Internet resources. This recipe will allow students and teachers to easily access multiple types of information in one central location to use as a portfolio or class web page.

Note: To include any of the content from the basic Google Tools, check out the recipe *Google Sites and Other Google Tools: Bringing Everything Together* (pages 35–37).

Skill

- Embed content from any source on the Internet and display it on a Google Sites page.

Ingredients

- Google Sites
- Blogger
- Feedly
- Google Calendar
- Google+
- RSS content from other sites
- Video, other than YouTube

 Preparations

- How to Create a Google Site (page 89)
- How to Create an Account with an RSS Widget Creator that Will Create an "iFrame" Tag to Embed RSS Feeds (page 120)

Coding in Google Sites: Getting Geeky (cont.)

Directions

1. RSS Include, 7thSpace iFrame Generator, and RSS Pump are a few sites that will allow you to create an iFrame tag from a blog feed. You can also use a tool like Tweetwally to generate an iFrame tag from your Twitter feed.

2. Create a Google site or navigate to a Google site that you have already created.

3. Edit the Google site by clicking on the **pencil** icon in the upper right-hand corner of the page.

4. Copy the code of the content you wish to embed into the site. This will be the "iFrame tag" that you created from RSS Include, 7thSpace iFrame Generator, or RSS Pump. As a general rule, Google Sites likes an iFrame tag to embed content. This will be a small piece of computer code. (See screenshot below for an example.)

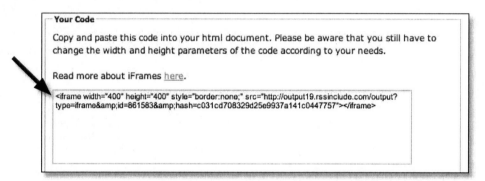

Your Code

Copy and paste this code into your html document. Please be aware that you still have to change the width and height parameters of the code according to your needs.

Read more about iFrames here.

```
<iframe width="400" height="400" style="border:none;" src="http://output19.rssinclude.com/output?type=iframe&amp;id=861583&amp;hash=c031cd708329d25e9937a141c0447757"></iframe>
```

5. Locate the place where the content is to be embedded into the Google Site and type in a series of repetitive letters, like this: "TTTTTTTTTTTTT." This will mark the spot.

6. Go to the top toolbar and click on the **<HTML> link** at the end of the toolbar.

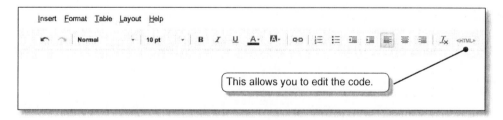

This allows you to edit the code.

Side Dish Recipes

7. A new window will appear with the HTML code of your Google site. Scroll down the code in the window and look for the series of letters you typed in your site. Once you have located the letters, click inside of the window at that point and paste the code for your content into the window. You can check your changes by clicking on the **Preview** tab. When you are ready to accept the changes, click the **Update** button.

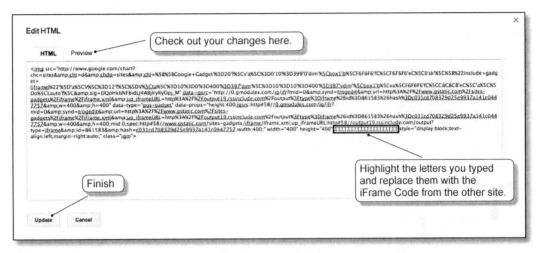

8. The content will now be embedded into the Google site. The size of the window and its justification (left, center, right) on the page can be edited by using the gadget editor (click on the **gear** of the gadget, while in edit mode) in Google Sites.

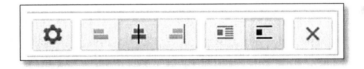

Serving Suggestions

- Develop content-specific project sites.
- Develop classroom sites.
- Create personal portfolios.

#51312—Creating a Google Apps™ Classroom

Google Maps: Collaborative Map Making

Description

In many subject areas, geography and history play a major part in the context of students' learning. Whether teachers want to have small groups trace a historical mathematician's life story, or want literature students to trace the travels of a particular character in a novel, collaborative map making is the solution.

Skills

- Create a map using Google Maps, and share and collaborate on the map with others.
- Add content, modify the look of the place markers, remix content, and add video to maps.
- Embed or link the entire map in a website or other digital work/artifact.

Ingredients

- Google Sites
- Google Maps

Preparations

- How to Embed a Google Map into a Google Site (page 94)
- How to Create a Google Map (page 96)
- How to Add Collaborators to a Google Map (page 97)
- How to Share a Google Map (page 98)
- How to Add Pins to a Google Map (page 99)
- How to Change Pins in a Google Map (page 101)
- How to Embed Multimedia Content into a Google Map (page 103)
- How to Draw Lines Between Locations in a Google Map (page 104)

Google Maps: Collaborative Map Making (cont.)

Directions

1. Have students create new maps with Google Maps. Add collaborators. Remember that the teacher should always be added as a collaborator.

2. Give the map a title and description. If different groups are working on the same topic, ask students to title their maps with unique identifiers.

3. Select whether the map will be public or unlisted. This can be changed later, but we suggest unlisted to start.

4. Have students choose locations to mark on the map. Enter an address in the search box and click **Save to Map**. Do this for all the locations to be marked.

5. There are tools that you can use to edit your map. These tools are located at the top of the map.

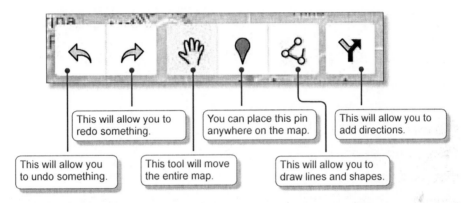

6. When all locations are entered on the map, have students return to **My Places** and click on the map. Place markers, lines, and other content can now be added.

7. Next, students should click on individual locations within their maps to change the default pins for the locations, embed multimedia content, or draw lines between locations.

8. When students have completed their maps, ask them to embed their maps into a shared Google site for viewing and sharing among the entire class, or for presentation purposes.

Serving Suggestions

- Trace a mathematician's life path.
- Create a map for your school's bus route.
- Trace the travels of literary characters.
- Create a map showing the migration of a society.
- Create a map of your classmates' summer vacations.

Google Drive: Searching and Evaluating
Resource Credibility

Description

Students are more connected to information than ever before via the Internet, but do they know how to find information? Can they evaluate the credibility of the resources they find? Teach students how to use Google Search to research effectively, and use a Google form to guide students through the process of evaluating those resources.

Skills

* Use Google Search effectively to find resources.
* Use Google Document to take notes.
* Evaluate resources to determine credibility using a Google form.

Ingredients

* Google Documents
* Google Search
* Google Forms
* Google Spreadsheets
* Google Presentation

Preparations

* How to Create a Google Form (page 75)
* How to Copy a Link to a Google Form (page 78)
* How to Create a Google Presentation (page 81)
* How to Upload a Google Presentation (page 82)

Directions

1. Locate helpful Google Search tips and resources to share with students.
2. Tell each student or group of students that they will be compiling their favorite search tips and tricks on Google documents titled "Google Search Tips: [Name]+[Period#]".

3. Direct students to helpful Google Search resources (like those listed below). Allow time for students to explore and document their findings. (Some sites have great visuals for you to print and display in your classroom.)

   - *Get More Out of Google*
     http://www.hackcollege.com/blog/2011/11/23/infographic-get-more-out-of-google.html

   - *Google Search Tips*
     http://static.googleusercontent.com/media/www.google.com/en/us/educators/posters/poster_search_tips_final.pdf

   - *Better searches. Better results.*
     https://drive.google.com/file/d/0B8tJGuc_3wooVUdfYWdWRUxiaDQ/edit?usp=sharing

   - *Anatomy of a Search.*
     http://foundation.aapg.org/library/googleWeb_Search.pdf

4. Once students have learned how to search more effectively, present them with an A Google A Day challenge. To find archived and categorized A Google A Day challenges, go to the *Google Search Education* website. http://www.google.com/insidesearch/searcheducation/lessons.html#challenges

5. Here you can view a collection of challenges labeled *culture*, *geography*, *history*, and *science*. Find the challenge you want to use with students and click **View challenge**. You will find the question as well as an explanation in a Google presentation.

6. Present the challenge to students. Allow students time to use Google Search to try to find the answer to the challenge. Remind students to use the search tips they documented on their Google docs.

7. Once students have had time to search and attempt to answer the question, you can go through the Google presentation with them to explain how to use Google Search to arrive at the answer. This may lead to a vibrant discussion about how different students approached the challenge.

8. After practicing with a couple of A Google A Day challenges, ask students to research a topic related to your class and find resources they think are reliable.

9. Ask students to complete a Google form that walks them through the process of evaluating an online resource.

Google Drive: Searching and Evaluating Resource Credibility *(cont.)*

10. Once you have opened this shared Google spreadsheet, click **File** and select **Make a copy**. Then, create your own copy of the spreadsheet.

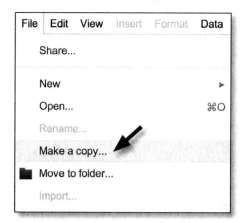

11. After making copies of this spreadsheet, click **Form** and choose **Go to live form** to share the link with students.

Serving Suggestion

- Teach students to gather and evaluate resources for both simple and more-sustained research assignments.

#51312—*Creating a Google Apps*™ *Classroom*

Google Drive: Analyzing Texts

Description

Teach students to shift from summarizing literary and informational texts to analyzing them and sharing their ideas with one another.

Skills

- Use a Google spreadsheet.
- Cite specific textual evidence.
- Analyze quotes, themes, events, characters, figurative language, etc.

Ingredients

- Google Drive and Google Spreadsheets

Preparations

- How to Create a Google Spreadsheet (page 79)
- How to Share a Google Document, Spreadsheet, or Presentation (page 83)

Directions

1. Navigate to the *Google Drive* website, and create a new spreadsheet.

2. Label the first row with directions for what students should add to each column. For example, the first column can be "Provide an example of a theme in the text. Include text citations." The second column can be labeled "Analyze the theme and explain how it develops in the text."

3. Once the spreadsheet has been properly labeled with the information students must add, click **Share** to share the spreadsheet with the class and select **can edit**. This will allow students to view and edit the shared spreadsheet, adding their citations and analysis, while also being able to read and learn from their peers' contributions.

Serving Suggestions

- Get English language arts students identifying and analyzing examples of figurative language.
- Engage an entire class in a prewriting exercise in preparation for an essay.
- Facilitate group analysis of historical documents (primary and secondary sources).

Google Alerts and Scholar:
Easy Research

Description

With the increase in project-based learning and an emphasis on connecting student work to real-life applications, this recipe allows students to use two simple tools to simultaneously gather information passively and actively.

Skills

- Gain access to primary-source materials easily.
- Be emailed every time a study topic has a new entry on the Internet.

Ingredients

- Google Alerts
- Google Search
- Google Scholar

Preparations

- How to Set Up a Google Alert (page 69)
- How to Use Advanced Search Skills (page 70)

Directions

1. Choose a research topic. Have students set up Google alerts for the topic. It is suggested that alerts be set to the specifications "Everything," "Once a Day," and "Only the Best Results," unless the instructions for the specific assignment require more specific information, like videos only. **Note:** There are Google alerts in Scholar and in the regular Google search engine.

Google Alerts and Scholar:
Easy Research *(cont.)*

2. Send students to the *Google Scholar* website.
   http://scholar.google.com

3. Instruct students to use advanced search skills (see page 70) by clicking on the down arrow to the right of the search box to find information on their topic.

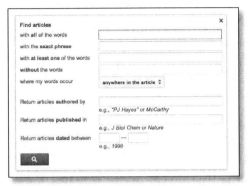

4. Once the Google Scholar search term is entered, remind students to look along the left-hand column of their results for more specialized search results, including legal proceedings and possible date ranges.

5. Students can narrow the search results even further by reviewing the **Cited by . . .** and **Related articles** hyperlinks underneath each individual article.

6. One easy way to create a bibliography or works cited page for the articles found is to use the free Google Apps™ for Education add-on/free website, *EasyBib*.
   http://www.easybib.com

7. Student researchers can use *EasyBib* to gather necessary information about the references they used and to provide that information with their final product.

8. When the research project is done, ask students to return to Google Alerts, click on **Manage your alerts** and delete the topic—unless there is a long-ranging interest in the topic—in which case, keep it!

Serving Suggestion

- Flip this recipe on its head and ask students to create a video or presentation about the best research practices.

Google Translate: Communicating with All Parents, Anytime, Anywhere

Description

In our global society, it has become increasingly necessary to be able to communicate across all language barriers on a regular basis. This is most true in our schools and classes, where the rich diversity of our students sometimes means challenges when communicating with their families. Using this recipe, teachers will find a simple, clear tool that can keep track of all communications with students' families, regardless of the languages that they speak.

Skills

- Practice multiple-language translations.
- See side-by-side translations to compare/contrast any information sent home.

Ingredients

- Google Search
- Google Translate

Preparations

- How to Upload a Google Document (page 72)
- How to Collaborate on a Google Document (page 73)
- How to Share a Google Document, Spreadsheet, or Presentation (page 83)

Google Translate: Communicating with All
Parents, Anytime, Anywhere (cont.)

Directions

1. Go to the *Google Translate* website.
   http://translate.google.com/toolkit

2. Below the text book, click on **translate a document**.

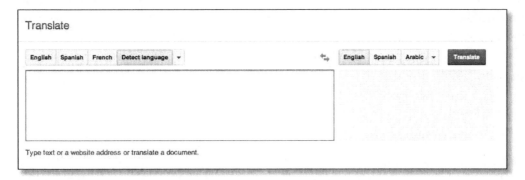

3. You will be prompted to choose a file from your computer. Click **Choose File**.

4. Once you have found your file to translate, click **choose**.

5. Click on the **Translate** button.

6. A new window or tab will open with your translated document. Copy and paste the text into Google Drive or other word processing program.

   - **Note:** If you are translating a document that is already saved in Google Drive, this process can be faster by opening the document, clicking on the **Tools** menu, and then clicking **Translate document**. Pick the preferred language for translation and click Translate. Now, you have a copy of the document, in the new language, saved to your Google Drive.

7. Proceed to email, or print the translated document for families to use.

Serving Suggestions

- Use a variation of this recipe by having students who are learning a language other than their native language practice their translation skills.

- Ask students to find an article or a website in another language and use the Translator Toolkit to translate it into their native language for primary and secondary source research.

#51312—*Creating a Google Apps™ Classroom*

YouTube and Goo.gl:
Multimedia QR Code Scaffolds

Description

As constructivist strategies such as project-based learning and inquiry-based learning become common practice in 21st century learning environments, the classroom environment is transforming into a community of learners, rather than a medium of information transfer. In such learning models, the instructor is more mobile, moving student-to-student and group-to-group, to help facilitate classroom activities. Using this side dish, students will be able to access strategically placed QR codes to view quick video tutorial hints on targeted misconceptions. This frees the teacher to spend additional time with struggling students, while simultaneously creating a rich learning resource library for students.

Skills

- Access a QR code via a mobile or computer device.
- Use an instructional video embedded in a QR code as a problem-solving scaffold.

Ingredients

- YouTube
- Goo.gl

Preparations

- How to Shorten a URL Using the Google URL Shortener (page 118)
- How to Resize a QR Code from the Google URL Shortener (page 119)

Directions

1. Create a document (hard copy or digital) that includes problems for students to solve.

YouTube and Goo.gl:
Multimedia QR Code Scaffolds *(cont.)*

2. Create a short instructional video with hints that target predicted areas in the assigned problem set where students will struggle.

   - Sites like *YouTube* or *Khan Academy* are excellent places to search for example videos produced by others.
     http://www.youtube.com/teachers
     http://www.khanacademy.org

3. Log into your YouTube account and upload your video to YouTube.

4. Copy the URL for your video. Navigate to **http://goo.gl** and shorten the URL.

5. Click on the **Details** link for the shortened URL to access the QR code.

6. Copy or drag the QR code image into your document. Place it in close proximity to the problem that is associated with the video hint embedded in the QR code.

Serving Suggestion

- Consider using QR code video scaffolds (videos that scaffold the understandings needed for students to engage in the activity prior to its start) and summative reviews upon the conclusion of chapters or units. Students will most likely be moving at varying paces on such activities.

Google Drawings:
Interactive Concept Maps

Description

Regardless of subject or discipline, progression through learning standards that cover all levels of Bloom's taxonomy requires not only content knowledge, but the ability to apply and connect various pieces of information in meaningful ways. Concept maps are useful, visual ways for students to create and observe the connectedness between various topics that at first look might appear disconnected. Using this side dish, students will learn to create concept maps using Google Drawings, and insert their maps into related documents. Using Google Drawings will allow for fluid peer-to-peer and instructor-to-peer sharing and commenting on the concept map.

Skills

- Create a concept map using Google Drawings.
- Insert the concept map into a related Google presentation.
- Share the concept map via Google Drive.

Ingredients

- Google Presentation
- Google Drawings
- Google Drive

Preparations

- How to Create a Google Document (page 71)
- How to Share a Google Document, Spreadsheet, or Presentation (page 83)
- How to Create and Insert a Google Drawing into a Google Document (page 85)

58

Google Drawings:
Interactive Concept Maps (cont.)

Directions

1. Prepare a list of topics within a unit of study that students are to organize via a concept map.

2. Show students various examples of concept maps and explain the process.

3. Instruct students to create a Google presentation that provides a written reflection about the connectedness between the topics from your list.

4. Have students turn written work into concept maps by creating Google drawings directly into slides of the presentation by using the Insert features (**Text Box**, **Image**, etc.).

5. Encourage students to include other multimedia in the presentation that supports their concept map.

6. Instruct students to share their concept map with peers and their teacher via Google Drive.

7. Instruct students to read and comment on one another's concept maps.

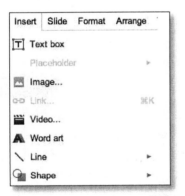

Serving Suggestions

- Use concept maps as an inquiry activity at the beginning of a unit to assess prior knowledge.
- Use concept maps as a summative activity to reinforce connectedness between topics.
- If one-to-one, encourage students to make simple concept maps at the conclusion of each class period.

Google Forms:
Create a Review Game Buzzer

Description

Review game competitions can be fun and motivating ways to prepare for assessments and review content. Often, review games are structured around questions in which the group who responds first wins. Determining which group actually "buzzes" their answer in first can be a difficult thing for teachers. Using this recipe, students will "buzz" their answer in using a Google form with their computer or mobile device. Because Google form responses are time stamped, the teacher will be able to assess immediately which group responded first.

Skill

- Respond to questions using a Google form.

Ingredients

- Google Forms and Google Spreadsheets

Preparations

- How to Create a Google Form (page 75)

Directions

1. Create a Google form. Include a space for each group to identify themselves and respond to the question. Set the type of question (i.e., multiple-choice, paragraph text) depending on the type of questions in the game.

2. Distribute the Google form to students during the review game.

3. Create a Google spreadsheet that collects the form responses and makes them visible during the game via a projector or whiteboard.

Serving Suggestions

- Use as a buzzer for extended review game activities.
- Use as a buzzer at the beginning of class for warm-up/opener responses.
- Use as a buzzer for exit ticket collection upon the conclusion of class.

YouTube: Create Your Own Adventure

Description

Have you ever seen a YouTube video that changes its course based on how the viewer interacts with it? With this recipe, students learn to create a video with multiple pathways that give different feedback to the viewer depending on how he or she answers questions. In addition, teachers can create video self-quizzes that help students get the learning they need, as they need it. This recipe will show how to create just this type of interactive video quiz.

Skills

- Create a YouTube video.
- Add links in a YouTube video.

Ingredient

- YouTube

 Preparations

- How to Create a YouTube Video (page 105)
- How to Add Annotations and Links in a YouTube Video (page 106)

Directions

1. Plan out the pathway for a Create Your Own Adventure activity. Any interactive video set will require at least four short videos.

    - The first (video A) explains a concept, asks a question, and offers a quiz question.

    - If the viewer answers A correctly, they will be linked to a final, congratulatory video (video D). If they answer incorrectly, they will be linked to a video (video B) with further instruction, that addresses the concept in a different way and asks the question again.

    - If the viewer answers B correctly, they will be taken to video C.

    - If they are incorrect on B, they can be given the option of viewing video A or video B again for further instruction. They can even be given a playlist of videos addressing the concept.

YouTube: Create Your Own Adventure *(cont.)*

2. Go to the *YouTube* website.
http://www.youtube.com

3. Log in using a Google account.

4. Click **Upload** at the top of the page.

5. Either upload your videos, or record your instructional videos directly from your webcam.

6. Once the videos are uploaded, add annotations and links to your videos, as appropriate.

7. Provide the initial video hyperlink to students and *voilà*! There is now a linked step-by-step self-quiz that can help any teacher personalize learning for any student.

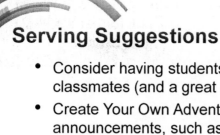

Serving Suggestions

- Consider having students create self-quizzes as a review project for their classmates (and a great resource for the teacher)!

- Create Your Own Adventure videos have been created as public service announcements, such as to warn against texting private information. Search for some of these videos and show them to students for inspiration.

- See this YouTube website for educational playlists that align with Common Core State Standards. http://www.youtube.com/teachers

Google+: Hanging Out with Experts

Description

Experts are all around us in virtual spaces! Give your students an opportunity to share their work with authors or experts around the world using Google Hangouts. Making students' work accessible worldwide gives an extra level of motivation and raises the quality of work. In addition, bringing experts into the classroom allows for real-life experiences and opportunities not previously afforded.

Skills

- Engage in meaningful real-world discussions with experts.
- Practice appropriate questioning procedures.

Ingredients

- Google+
- Google Drive
- Google Documents

Preparations

- How to Create a Google Document (page 71)
- How to Collaborate on a Google Document (page 73)
- How to Share a Google Document, Spreadsheet, or Presentation (page 83)
- How to Research Using Google+ (page 107)
- How to Start a Google+ Hangout (page 109)
- How to Broadcast a Google+ Hangout Using Hangouts On Air (page 110)
- How to Screen Share in a Google+ Hangout (page 113)

Google+: Hanging Out with Experts *(cont.)*

Directions

1. Create a document about a teacher-directed particular learning topic and share it with all students.

2. On the document, begin a running list of questions about the topic.

3. Instruct students how to research using Google+ and add resources to the shared document, adding questions as resources are added. You may choose to structure the document ahead of time with a two-column table—one column for resources and one column for questions.

4. Search for, and collaboratively decide on, a list of "top three experts" (who have Google+ profiles) with whom the class would like to have a discussion.

5. Contact the three experts and propose a panel discussion via Google+ Hangouts with your class.

6. When the experts are confirmed and the time and date is set for the panel discussion, prepare students by categorizing questions based on theme.

   - Choose at least two opening questions for the panel, and assign questions to various students, maintaining as much equity as possible in assigning such questions.

   - Also, leave at least 10 minutes at the end of the discussion for general Q&A (or Q&A from the wider Google+ audience, if you choose to make this a Hangout On-Air).

7. Now, publicize! Especially if you choose to have the Hangout On-Air, make sure to publicize the upcoming Hangout on Google+, other social networks, and through the school.

8. Afterward, make sure students write thank-you notes to the experts and complete a teacher-directed culminating activity (e.g., students could create video recordings of themselves talking about what they learned in the process).

Serving Suggestions

- If using this with upper grades, give students much more ownership in terms of researching and connecting with the expert(s).
- For English language arts, consider finding authors to discuss the craft of writing.

Google Presentations:
Quickly Digitize Student Work

Description

Whether you are in a one-to-one classroom or you are a teacher trying to create a paperless learning environment, finding a fluid way to assign and collect student work can be a challenge. In particular, subjects such as science and math that require drawing unique symbols and formulas and performing various calculations can make creating work using only digital tools (laptop, iPad, etc.) difficult. Using this recipe, students will create work on paper as they normally would and take a picture within Google Presentations or Documents to submit and use as a drop box. Moreover, uploaded work can be easily shared with peers within and across classes.

Skills

- Use paper and a writing utensil to perform a task (e.g., solve or create a problem, compose writing).
- Take a picture of work using the snapshot tool and embed the image in Google Presentations to a particular slide or into a Google Document.
- Share uploaded work with instructor and peers.

Ingredients

- Google Drive
- Google Presentations

 Preparations

- How to Create a Google Presentation (page 81)
- How to Upload a Google Presentation (page 82)
- How to Share a Google Document, Spreadsheet, or Presentation (page 83)
- How to Take a Snapshot in Google Documents or Google Presentations (page 88)

65

Google Presentations:
Quickly Digitize Student Work *(cont.)*

Directions

1. Instruct students to create a Google document or Google presentation using Google Drive.

2. Assign a written task.

3. Instruct students to turn in their written task by taking a snapshot of their work and inserting that image into a slide in their Google presentation.

4. Instruct students to share their work with their instructor and peers (if desired).

Serving Suggestions

- Use as a drop box or portfolio for all work upon conclusion of a chapter or unit.
- Use as a drop box to collect work on a daily basis.

#51312—Creating a Google Apps™ Classroom

Preparations

Preparations

How to
Set Up a Google Alert

❶ Sign into your Google account. Go to the *Google Alerts* website.
http://google.com/alerts

❷ Enter a search term into the first box, and the sample results will automatically be shown in the box to the right.

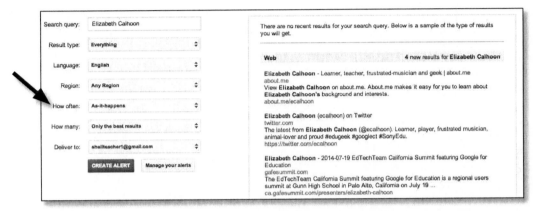

❸ It is recommended that the result type, frequency, number, and delivery method remain as the default, with the exception of **How Often**. In the image above, the **How Often** field has been changed from **Once a Day** to **As-it-happens**. Choose your preference as to how often you would like to be notified.

❹ Click **Create Alert**.

❺ If you ever want to adjust your Google Alerts, follow these steps:

- Sign into your Google account.

- Return to the *Google Alerts* website.
  http://google.com/alerts

- Click on **Manage your alerts**.

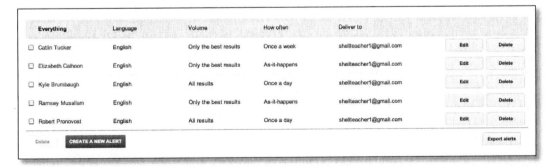

How to
Use Advanced Search Skills

❶ Sign into your Google account.

❷ If you are searching for information, go to the *Google Advanced Search* website.
https://www.google.com/advanced_search

❸ If you are searching for images, go to the the *Google Advanced Image Search* website.
https://www.google.com/advanced_image_search

❹ In plain English, use the prompts to specify your exact desired search.

❺ Be sure to review all of the options, including SafeSearch, reading level, and usage rights.

How to
Create a Google Document

❶ Sign into your Google account. Go to the *Google Drive* website. **https://drive.google.com**

❷ Click the red button titled **Create** and select **Document**.

How to
Upload a Google Document

❶ Sign into your Google account. Go to the *Google Drive* website.
https://drive.google.com

❷ Click the red upload icon directly to the right of the red button titled **Create**.

❸ Choose the file or folder you would like to upload.

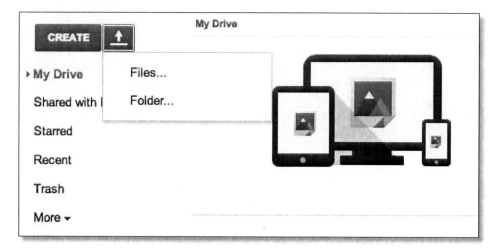

How to
Collaborate on a Google Document

❶ Sign into your Google account. Go to the *Google Drive* website. **https://drive.google.com**

❷ When someone is viewing or editing a Google document at the same time as you, a colored tile with their name or an anonymous symbol will appear in the top of your screen. Real-time collaboration can happen in a document, spreadsheet, presentation, or drawing. However, collaboration does not need to happen in real time.

❸ Click on the colored tiles and a chat box will appear for instant messaging between collaborators.

❹ If different collaborators are editing a document at the same time, cursors will appear with the colors and names of the collaborators.

How to
Make a Google Document into a Template

❶ Sign into your Google account. Go to the *Google Drive* website. **https://drive.google.com**

❷ Select the document you wish to use as a template from the list in your drive by clicking on the empty box to the left of the title of the document.

❸ Checking the box will make a menu appear across the top of the list. Click on **More**, then click **Submit to template gallery**.

❹ On the next page, enter a description for the template and choose its category(s) and language. Then, click **Submit template**.

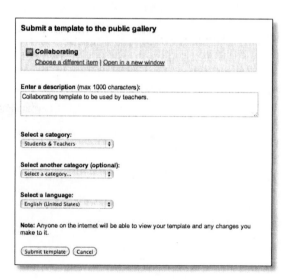

How to
Create a Google Form

❶ Sign into your Google account. Go to the *Google Drive* website. **https://drive.google.com**

❷ Click the red button titled **Create** and select **Form**.

❸ Give your form a name, and choose a theme.

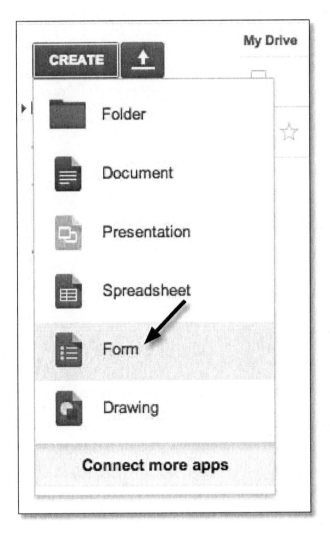

How to
Add Questions to a Google Form

❶ Sign into your Google account. Go to the *Google Drive* website. **https://drive.google.com**

❷ Once you have created a form in Google docs, named it, and chosen a theme, the form will open on a page where you can type your first question. Enter your question in the **Question Title** box.

❸ Below the Question Title box is a drop-down menu titled **Question Type**. This menu will allow you to choose from several different formats for your question.

   • Text—Allows for short (one sentence) responses.

   • Paragraph text—Allows for a response up to 5,000 characters.

   • Multiple choice—Allows for only one response and can be used to send users to another section of your form. (Logic)

   • Check boxes—Allows respondents to select multiple items.

   • Choose from a list—This provides a drop-down menu for users to select the item they want. (Does not allow for logic.)

   • Scale—Allows the use of a "Likert Scale" (1–5).

   • Grid—Allows the use of rows and columns in a grid arrangement.

   • Date—Allows the user to specify a particular date.

   • Time—Allows the user to specify a particular time.

❹ Click the blue **Done** button when you have finished designing your question.

❺ If you wish to add another question, click on the **Add item** button. You can then choose the same question format you used before, or a different style.

❻ If you wish to create a custom layout, separate certain questions from others, group questions on one page, or provide content to go with your question, click on the small arrow button next to Add item. There you will see layout options.

   • Section header—Allows the user to create a header to a specific group of items in the form.

   • Page break—Allows the user to allocate items to specific pages in the form.

How to
Add Questions to a Google Form *(cont.)*

- Image—Allows the user to add an image to the form directly.
- Video—Allows the user to add a video to the form directly.

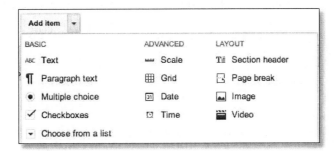

❼ If you want to edit, copy, or delete any of your questions, you can use the small menu on the right-hand side of the question.

❽ When you are finished with each question, click on the blue **Done** button. Next to the **Done** button there is also a check box that says, **Required question**. If you check this box, your respondents will not be able to successfully click **Submit** at the end of the form unless this question has been answered.

❾ Next, you can choose where the data entered into the form will go. By default, two files will be placed in your Google drive—one will have just the name of your form and the other will have the name of your form followed by **(Responses)**. You can choose to have the data collected inside another spreadsheet (the default), inside the form itself, or as a new sheet inside an existing spreadsheet. Click **Choose response destination** from the choices across the top of the page to format these settings.

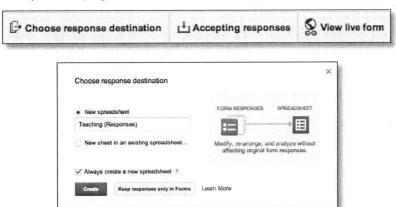

© *Shell Education* #51312—*Creating a Google Apps™ Classroom*

How to
Copy a Link to a Google Form

❶ Sign into your Google account. Go to the *Google Drive* website.
https://drive.google.com

❷ Open your Google form—it will open in spreadsheet view.

❸ Look at the choices at the top of the page and select **View live form**.

❹ Click on the URL in your web address bar and highlight the entire web address.

❺ Use CTRL+C (Windows) or CMND+C (Macintosh) to copy the link/URL.

❻ Use CTRL+V (Windows) or CMND+V (Macintosh) to paste the link/URL to your destination.

How to
Create a Google Spreadsheet

❶ Sign into your Google account. Go to the *Google Drive* website. **https://drive.google.com**

❷ Click the red button titled **Create** and select **Spreadsheet**.

❸ Click on the gray, italicized words **Untitled spreadsheet** to give the spreadsheet a title.

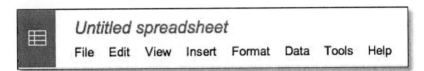

How to
Insert a Script into a Google Spreadsheet

❶ Sign into your Google account. Go to the *Google Drive* website. **https://drive.google.com**

❷ Open a new or previously created spreadsheet.

❸ Once you have entered data in your spreadsheet, go to the Insert drop-down menu and select **Script**.

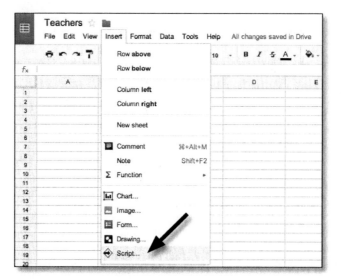

❹ You can choose to browse the scripts available in the **Script Gallery** or search for the title of a specific script.

❺ Once you have found the script you would like to use, click **Install**.

❻ This process may take you through a couple of steps. Follow the on-screen directions.

How to
Create a Google Presentation

❶ Sign in to your Google Drive account. Go to the *Google Drive* website. **https://drive.google.com**

❷ Click the red button titled **Create** and select **Presentation**.

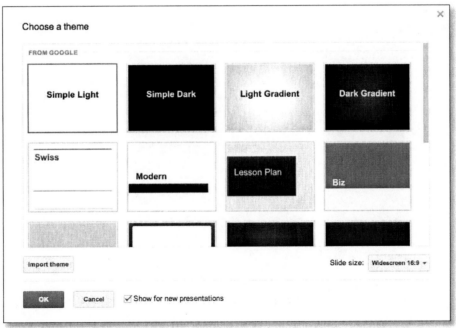

How to
Upload a Google Presentation

❶ Sign in to your Google Drive account. Go to the *Google Drive* website.
https://drive.google.com

❷ Click the red upload icon directly to the right of the red button titled **Create**.

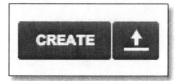

❸ Choose the file you would like to upload.

How to
Share a Google Document, Spreadsheet, or Presentation

❶ Sign into your Google account. Go to the *Google Drive* website. **https://drive.google.com**

❷ Open the document, spreadsheet, or presentation you wish to share.

❸ Click on the blue **Share** button on the top right of the page.

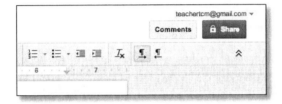

❹ In the **Invite people** text box at the bottom of the page, enter the email addresses of the individual(s) with whom you wish to share the item.

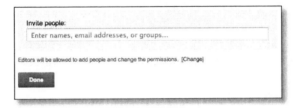

❺ When you enter the email address of the individual(s) with whom you wish to share, a drop-down menu will appear to the right. By clicking on this link, you can set the sharing settings.

❻ If you wish to notify the individuals that you have shared this item with them, leave the **Notify people via email** box checked. Otherwise, remove the check. At this time, you may also click the **Add message** hyperlink to add your own message to the email.

How to
Share a Google Document, Spreadsheet, or Presentation *(cont.)*

❼ Alternately, if you want to share the document, spreadsheet, or presentation with a larger group, you can click on the blue **Change** link.

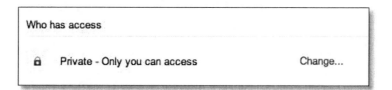

❽ Select the sharing options desired; you can make the item available to the entire Internet or just to people who have the specific link. You can also change the access options as you did in step 6. Be sure to click on the green **Save** button when you have finished your selections.

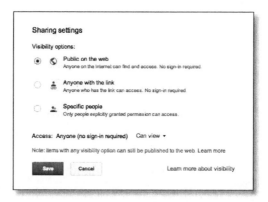

❾ You will return to the previous screen, but you will see that the access settings have been changed. Now, you can share the item with anyone by sending a copy of the link/URL in the **Link to share** box.

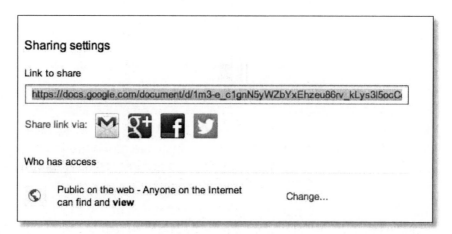

How to
Create and Insert a Google Drawing into a Google Document

❶ Sign into your Google account. Go to the *Google Drive* website.
https://drive.google.com

❷ Open a previously created document or click the red button titled **Create** and select **Document** to create a new document.

❸ Once you have opened your document, go to the Insert drop-down menu and select **Drawing**.

❹ Create your drawing using the options available along the top of the drawing box. It may take some practice to become proficient with the tools. When you have finished your drawing, click **Save & Close**.

❺ Your drawing should now appear in your document. By clicking on the drawing, you can easily change its size and how it aligns with the text.

How to
Create a Google Folder

❶ Sign into your Google account. Go to the *Google Drive* website.
   https://drive.google.com

❷ Click the red button titled **Create** and select **Folder**.

❸ Give your folder a name.

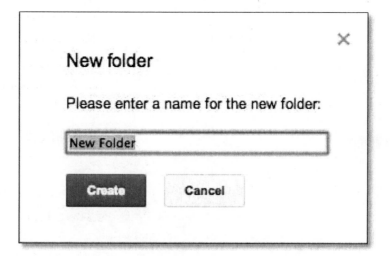

#51312—Creating a Google Apps™ Classroom   © *Shell Education*

How to
Share a Google Folder

❶ Sign into your Google account. Go to the *Google Drive* website.
https://drive.google.com

❷ On the vertical bar on the left of the screen, click the arrow to the left of My Drive to view the folders you have created and want to share.

❸ Hover over the folder you want to share and right click on the arrow to the right of the folder's name to view a menu.

❹ Click on **Share**.

❺ Under **Invite people**, enter the email addresses of the individuals with whom you would like to share the folder.

❻ Choose their editing rights to the right of their email addresses.

❼ If you wish to notify the individuals that you have shared this folder with them, leave the **Notify people via email** box checked. Otherwise, remove the check. At this time you may also click the **Add message** hyperlink to add your own message to the email. If you want to share the folder with a larger group, you can click on the blue **Change** link.

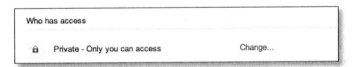

❽ Select the sharing options desired; you can make the folder available to the entire Internet or just to people who have the specific link. You can also change the access options as you did in step 7. Click on **Save**.

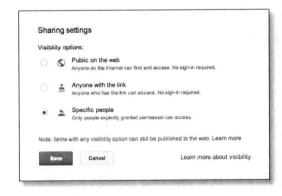

❾ You will return to the previous screen, but will see that the access settings have been changed and you can share the folder with anyone by sending a copy of the link/URL in the **Link to share** box.

How to
Take a Snapshot in Google Documents or Presentations

❶ Sign into your Google account. Go to the *Google Drive* website. **https://drive.google.com**

❷ Open a new or previously created document or presentation.

- **Note:** Since a snapshot is a quick picture, you can only take one shot at a time. If you are taking a picture of a two-page or more document or presentation, you will need to take multiple snapshots.

❸ Go to the Insert menu.

❹ Choose **Image**.

❺ Choose **Take a snapshot**.

- **Note:** Depending on the type of computer you are using, you may be prompted to allow the camera access to various features such as taking a snapshot. Enable that access, as needed.

How to
Create a Google Site

❶ Sign into your Google account. Go to the *Google Sites* website.
https://sites.google.com

❷ Click on the red **Create** button.

- It is suggested that you use a **Blank template** (use pre-fabricated templates for inspiration, but you will have much more freedom of where items are placed on your site if you start with a blank template).

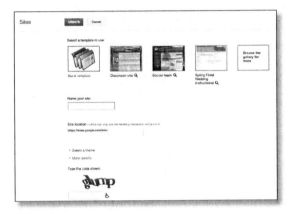

❸ Name your site. The URL for your site will be created automatically based on what you name your site.

❹ Select a theme for your site (this can be changed at any time).

❺ Click on **More options** and describe your site.

❻ Type in the CAPTCHA code as indicated on the site creation page.

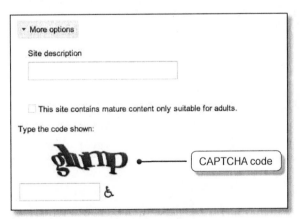

❼ Click the **Create Site** button at the top of the page.

- It is possible that the URL that is automatically generated for you may already be in use. If so, Google will be unable to create your site until you experiment with other URL possibilities and find an option that is available.

How to
Share and Collaborate
on a Google Site

❶ Sign into your Google account. Go to the *Google Sites* website. **https://sites.google.com**

❷ Click on the site that you would like to share.

❸ Click on the blue **Share** button in the upper right-hand corner.

❹ You will be taken to the Manage Site page.

❺ At the bottom, where it says **Invite people**, type in any email address, choose if that person will be an owner (can change all settings), an editor (can change the content of any page on the site), or a viewer (they can only view the site), and that person will get an email informing them that they have been added to the site. Click the **Add message** hyperlink if you wish to add anything to this form email.

❻ Additionally, you can set the access settings for your site on the Manage Site page. Google sites have a default public setting. If you wish to make your site private or semi-private, click on **Change** and alter the visibility options.

• **Note:** You can also enable page-level permissions. To enable these, click on the **Enable page-level permissions** button in the upper right-hand corner when you are on the Manage Site page. From there, different individuals can be made editors on individual pages.

How to
Create a Page in Google Sites

❶ Sign into your Google account. Go to the *Google Sites* website. **https://sites.google.com**

❷ Click on the site on which you'd like to add a page.

❸ Click on the button at the top right that has a **+** sign on it.

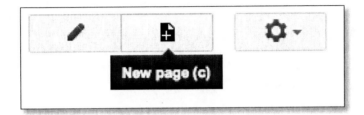

❹ Name your page.

❺ Choose which type of page you'd like to use. If you'd like to learn more about the details of each type of page, click on **Learn more** next to the drop-down menu that allows you to choose the type of page. A guide to the different pages will be displayed.

❻ Under **Select a location**, choose how the new page will be listed on the sidebar on your site's home page. It can appear at the top level (in line with your home page), as a sub-page of your home page, or in a different location (different locations may be used when you begin to have multiple pages on one website).

❼ Click the red **Create** button at the top of the page. Your new page will come up, and you can proceed to type materials, add files or links, and create the content.

❽ If you would like to change the layout of the pages or of the sidebar that lists the pages, click on the **gear** drop-down menu while viewing any page on your site.

- Click on **Edit site layout**.
- Make any edits from this location. You are encouraged to try out different layouts and preview the different looks before saving.

How to
Embed a Google Document into a Google Site

❶ Sign into your Google account. Go to the *Google Drive* website.
https://drive.google.com

❷ Make sure the document that you want to embed in your site is in your Google Drive/Docs list. If it is not, upload the document into your drive and make sure it is **Public** so that it can be viewable by anyone who visits your site. **Note:** See pages 83–84 for how to make a document public.

❸ Go to the Google Sites website.
https://sites.google.com

❹ Open the site that you want to edit.

❺ Navigate to the page that will have the document embedded into it.

❻ Click on the **Edit page** button (it looks like a pencil) in the upper right-hand corner of the page.

❼ Click on the **Insert** drop-down menu in the upper left-hand corner of the screen.

❽ Look for the word **Drive** in the menu and click the arrow next to it. More options will appear. Choose **Document**.

❾ Choose the document you would like to embed. If you have many documents, it may be most useful to enter the title of your document in the search box at the top of the list.

  • **Note:** You can also choose to embed a presentation, spreadsheet, form, video, drawing, folder, calendar, map, photo, or photo album from this location!

❿ Click on the chosen document and click the blue **Select** button.

⓫ Choose whether you want a border and/or a title for your document, and adjust its width and height. The default options are best to keep as is for beginner users.

⓬ Click **Save**.

⓭ You will not be able to view the document as it will appear on your site until you save the page itself. Click the blue **Save** button in the top corner of the page and adjust to your preferences.

How to
Embed a YouTube Video into a Google Site

❶ Sign into your Google account. Go to the *Google Sites* website. **https://sites.google.com**

❷ Open the site that you want to edit.

❸ Navigate to the page that will have the video embedded into it.

❹ Click on the **Edit page** button (it looks like a pencil) in the upper right-hand corner of the page.

❺ Click on the **Insert** drop-down menu in the upper left-hand corner of the screen.

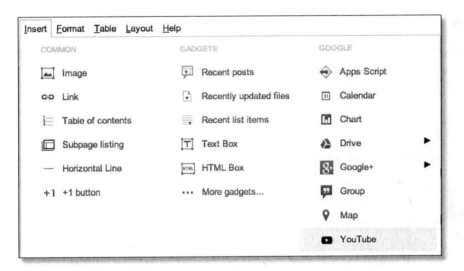

❻ On the drop-down menu, look for the word **YouTube** and click on it.

❼ Paste or type the URL of the YouTube video in the field provided.

❽ Choose whether you want a border and/or a title for your video and adjust its size.

❾ Click **Save**.

❿ You will not be able to view the video itself as it will appear on your site until you save the page itself. Click the blue **Save** button in the top corner of the page and adjust to your preferences.

How to
Embed a Google Map into a Google Site

❶ Sign into your Google account. Go to the *Google Sites* website. **https://sites.google.com**

❷ Open the site that you want to edit.

❸ Navigate to the page that will have the map embedded into it.

❹ Click on the **Edit page** button (it looks like a pencil) in the upper right-hand corner of the page.

❺ Click on the **Insert** drop-down menu in the upper left-hand corner.

❻ Look for the word **Map** and click on it.

❼ If you want to include a map with just one location, enter the location in the field at the top of the box.

❽ If you want to include a link to a map, paste the URL to that map in the field at the bottom of the box.

❾ If you want to include one of your own personalized maps, click on **My Maps** in the left-hand column.

❿ Your list of maps will be shown. Click on the map you want to embed.

⓫ Click **Select**.

⓬ Choose whether you want a border and/or a title for your map, and adjust its width and height. Keep the default options as is if you are a beginner.

⓭ Click **Save**.

⓮ You will not be able to view the map itself as it will appear on your site until you save the page itself. Click the blue **Save** button in the top corner of the page and adjust to your preferences.

How to
Embed a Gadget into a Google Site

❶ Sign into your Google account. Go to the *Google Sites* website.
https://sites.google.com

❷ Open the site that you want to edit.

❸ Navigate to the page that will have the gadget embedded into it.

❹ Click on the **Edit page** button in the upper right-hand corner of the page.

❺ Click on the **Insert** drop-down menu in the upper left-hand corner of the screen.

❻ Look for the term **More gadgets** and click on it.

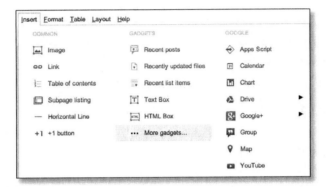

❼ A pop-up box will provide a list of prefabricated gadgets to embed. Gadgets can include communication tools, various games, and much more.

❽ Choose your gadget and click **Select**.

❾ You will be given a variety of options regarding the appearance and use of the gadget. Adjust these to your preferences and click **OK**.

❿ You will not be able to view the gadget itself as it will appear on your site until you save the page itself. Click **Save** and adjust to your preferences.

95

How to
Create a Google Map

❶ Sign into your Google account. Go to the *Google Maps* website.
http://maps.google.com

❷ Click in the search box in the upper left-hand corner of the screen and a link to **My custom maps** will appear. Click on this link and a new box will appear.

❸ Click on the **pencil** icon to the right to create a new map.

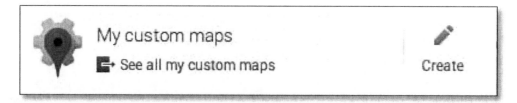

❹ Give your new map a title by clicking on **Untitled map**. Add a description if needed. Click **Save**.

 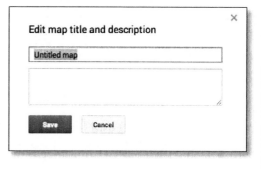

- **Note:** Visit this site for a video and tutorial, produced by Google, that gives an overview of creating custom maps.
http://goo.gl/1KPY9

How to
Add Collaborators to a Google Map

❶ Sign in to your Google account. Go to the *Google Maps* website. **http://maps.google.com**

❷ Click in the search box in the upper left-hand corner of the screen and a link to **My custom maps** will appear. Click on this link and a new box will appear.

❸ Select your map from the list and then click **Open original map**. Alternately, you can access your maps by clicking on the **gear** icon in the lower right corner of the main maps page.

❹ Click the green **Share** button, which is in the upper right-hand corner of the map. Google Maps follows the same sharing procedures that other Google tools use. Public maps are shared with everyone and are published in search results and surface in the user profile. Unlisted maps are only shared with people who have the URL or who are granted access. Click **Change** if you wish to alter the visibility options from the public default.

❺ If you wish to invite specific people to view your map, enter email addresses in the box titled **Invite people**. To the right of the email box, select whether each person will be allowed to edit or simply view the map. Decide whether you would like to send emails to notify people that they have been added to this map (the default) and also whether you would like to add a personal message to the form emails.

❻ Click the **Send** button when you are finished inviting collaborators.

How to
Share a Google Map

❶ Sign into your Google account. Go to the *Google Maps* website.
http://maps.google.com

❷ Click in the search box in the upper left-hand corner of the screen and a link
to **My custom maps** will appear. Click on this link and a new box will appear.
Select your map from the list. Alternately, you can access your maps by
clicking on the **gear** icon in the lower right corner of the main maps page.

❸ Click on the **gear** icon in the lower right-hand side of the map and select
Share and embed map.

❹ A pop-up box will appear, which will display the link and the embed code.

❺ Copy and paste the URL to send to someone via email or copy and paste the
HTML code to embed the map into a website.

Note: Check the **Short URL** box to make the link more manageable.

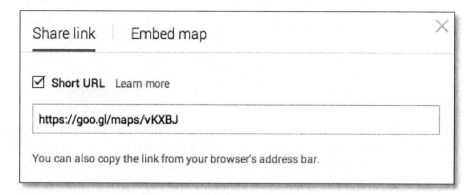

❻ Click the **X** in the upper right corner of the pop-up to close the window.

How to
Add Pins to a Google Map

❶ Sign into your Google account. Go to the *Google Maps* website.
   http://maps.google.com

❷ Click in the search box in the upper left-hand corner of the screen and a link
   to **My custom maps** will appear. Click on this link and a new box will appear.
   Select your map from the list and then click **Open original map**. Alternately,
   you can access your maps by clicking on the **gear** icon in the lower right
   corner of the main maps page.

❸ Select the **Add marker** pin tool from the menu just under the search bar.

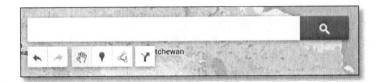

❹ Click anywhere on the map to place the pin.

❺ Drag the pin to a specific location on the map.

❻ Unclick or "drop" the pin once it is positioned where you want it. A window
   will open.

❼ Create a title and description (or address) for the pin. In the editing box, you
   can choose plain text, rich text, or to edit the html.

How to
Add Text to a Google Map

❶ Sign into your Google account. Go to the *Google Maps* website.
   http://maps.google.com

❷ Click in the search box in the upper left-hand corner of the screen and a link
   to **My custom maps** will appear. Click on this link and a new box will appear.
   Select your map from the list and then click **Open original map**. Alternately,
   you can access your maps by clicking on the **gear** icon in the lower right
   corner of the main maps page.

❸ Click on a pin. Then, click on the **Edit** button to enter editing mode for the
   chosen map.

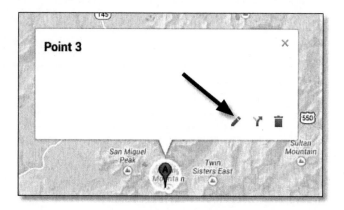

❹ In the **Title** field, provide a name and description (or address) for the pin.
   In the editing box, you can choose Plain text, rich text, or to edit the html.

❺ Click on any of the pins on the map and a window will open. Click on the
   pencil icon to edit the information attached to the pin. You can edit the
   location name and other information about the location from this window. By
   clicking on the camera icon, you can also add images and videos to the pin.

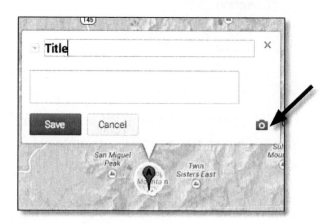

How to
Change Pins in a Google Map

❶ Sign into your Google account. Go to the *Google Maps* website. **http://maps.google.com**

❷ Locate the text box in the upper left corner of the map, click inside the box and a link to **My custom maps** will appear. Click on this link and a new box will appear. Select your map from the list and then click **Open original map.** Alternately, you can access your maps by clicking on the **gear** icon in the lower right corner of the main maps page.

❸ From the list of pins on your map, click on the **paint bucket** icon to the right of the item on the list.

❹ There will be a pop-up next to the list of pins that will allow you to change the pin icon, type, color, or transparency. At the bottom of this pop-up, there is a **More Icons** button to select different icons.

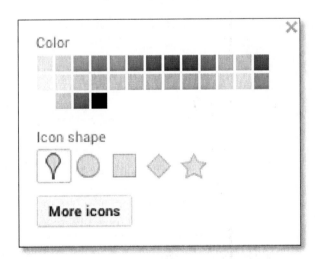

❺ Click on the **pencil** icon to add descriptive information.

How to
Change Pins in a Google Map *(cont.)*

❻ You can change or add the following:

- The title of the location

- The description of the location, a link to any information you would like to add to the pin within the text box, and place details, including address, phone, website, and category.

❼ Click **Save**.

How to
Embed Multimedia Content into a Google Map

❶ Sign into your Google account. Go to the *Google Maps* website. http://maps.google.com

❷ Click in the search box in the upper left-hand corner of the screen and a link to **My custom maps** will appear. Click on this link and a new list will appear. Select your map from the list and then click **Open original map**. Alternately, you can access your maps by clicking on the **gear** icon in the lower right corner of the main Maps page.

❸ Click on any **pin** on the map and a window will open. Click on the **pencil** icon to edit the information attached to the pin. You can add text, links, images, and videos to the pin. You can also edit the location name and other information about the location from this window.

❹ Add images and videos by adding the URL of the image or YouTube video. This will allow you to create your own slideshow for the location. You may add a maximum of 10 items.

❺ Remember to click **Save** on the pop-up box. The pin should now be changed on the map and on your list of locations on the left-hand side of your map.

How to
Draw Lines Between Locations in a Google Map

❶ Sign into your Google account. Go to the *Google Maps* website.
http://maps.google.com

❷ Click in the search box in the upper left-hand corner of the screen and a link to **My custom maps** will appear. Click on this link and a new box will appear. Select your map from the list and then click **Open original map**. Alternately, you can access your maps by clicking on the **gear** icon in the lower right corner of the main Maps page.

❸ Click on the **Draw a line** tool from the menu just under the search bar.

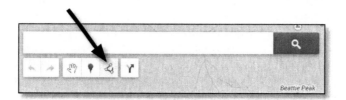

❹ Place the crosshairs on the map and single click and hold to begin the line, then drag the line to the next location. A black line will appear between your start point and end point. If you want your line to have only one segment, double-click again on your end point to finish the line. If you want your line to have multiple segments, continue to create segments until you are done, and then double-click again on the last point to finish.

❺ When you finish your line and double-click off the end point, an information box will come up automatically. It is identical to the one used for pins, and allows you to name your line and enter a description.

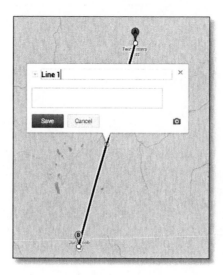

How to
Create a YouTube Video

❶ Sign into your Google account. Go to the *YouTube* website.
https://www.youtube.com

❷ Click on the **Upload** button at the top of the page.

❸ If you already have a video file on your computer, follow the step-by-step instructions on the page to upload the video.

❹ If you want to create a new video using your webcam, click on the **Record** button under **Webcam capture** on the right side of the screen.

❺ Ensure that Adobe Flash Player Settings are enabled (click **Remember** for ease in the future). **Note:** Be sure to discuss with students the importance of using the privacy settings.

❻ Your webcam should automatically turn on and you should be able to see your image in the box on the screen.

❼ Click on the button on the bottom that says **Start recording**.

❽ When you are done, click **Stop recording** and choose to either **Start over** or **Upload**.

❾ Choose the title, description, and details for your video.

❿ Once the video is uploaded, go to YouTube Editor to mash-up videos and add annotations, titles, copyright-free music, and transitions.
http://www.youtube.com/editor

• **Note:** There are a variety of other tools you can use within YouTube to create videos. They can be found at a special location within YouTube. **http://www. youtube.com/yt/creators/tools.html**

How to
Add Annotations and Links in a YouTube Video

❶ Sign into your Google account. Go to the *YouTube* website. **https://www.youtube.com**

❷ Upload an existing video or create a new video on YouTube.

❸ Click on the small drop-down menu next to the **Upload** button and select **Video Manager**.

❹ Click on the drop-down menu next to the **Edit** button that sits next to the video you want to annotate and select **Annotations**.

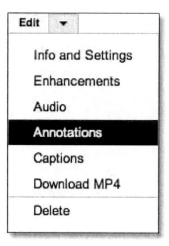

❺ Drag the slider bar at the bottom of the page to the precise place in the video where you would like your annotation.

❻ Click the **Add Annotation** button in the top right-hand part of the page.

❼ Select **Note**.

❽ Type your annotation in the box provided and make any edits to the text, like font size, font color, or background color.

❾ If you would like to make your annotation into a link, click on the **Link** box.

❿ Choose what you would like the annotation to link to, such as another video, a playlist, or something else, from the drop-down menu.

⓫ Paste or type in the URL to the target video.

⓬ Once you have made all of the customizations to your liking, remember to click the blue **Publish** button in the upper right corner of the screen.

How to
Research Using Google+

❶ Sign into your Google account. Go to the *Google+* website.
https://plus.google.com

❷ Click in the search box at the top of the page.

❸ Search for a topic. For the best result, use a hashtag (#) before your search term, such as #election or #Olympics.

❹ You can refine your search by using the list of items in the **Trending** box that appears.

     #51312—Creating a Google Apps™ Classroom

How to

Post a Local Business Review in Google+

❶ Sign into your Google account. Go to the *Google+* website. **https://plus.google.com**

❷ Click on **Home** on the left-hand side and a drop-down menu will appear. Select **Local**.

❸ Search for the business you want to review by entering the business name and location in the text box at the top of the page.

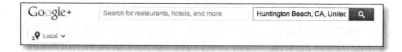

❹ From the search list, find the business you would like to review.

❺ Click the **pencil** icon to write a review of the business.

❻ Rate different aspects of the place using the 0 (poor) to 5 (excellent) star scale, and write any information that you think will be helpful in the text box.

❼ When you are done, click **Publish**. Any reviews that you write will be public and will be attributed to your Google+ name.

How to
Start a Google+ Hangout

❶ Sign into your Google account. Go to the *Google+* website.
   https://plus.google.com

❷ Click on **Hangouts** in the upper right-hand corner.

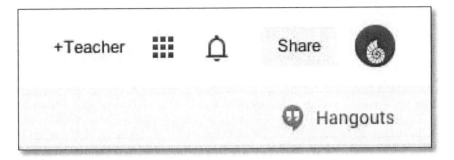

❸ By clicking on the plus sign at the top of the box that appears, you can enter names or email addresses to search for people you know. Select those people to add them to your Hangout list.

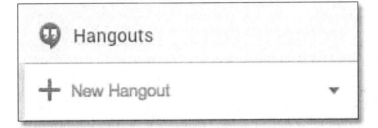

❹ Look at the bottom of your list of contacts. Click on **Start a video hangout**.

❺ A new window will pop up. You may be prompted to enable your audio and video. Enable features, as needed.

❻ You will then be given a link to share to have others join your hangout, or you can invite people explicitly via email addresses or phone numbers.

❼ The green **Invite** button will be disabled until at least one other person has been invited.

❽ If you want to try Hangouts without anyone else so that you can just explore the options, click Cancel and your Hangout pop-up window will still be there for you to explore the options and features before inviting others.

How to
Broadcast a Google+ Hangout Using Hangouts On Air

❶ Sign into your Google account. You must also have created a YouTube channel in order to broadcast a Google+ Hangout. Go to the *Google+* website. **https://plus.google.com**

❷ Click on **Home** and a drop-down menu will appear. Select **Hangouts**.

❸ Click **Start a Hangout On Air**.

❹ Name the Hangout. This name will be the title of the YouTube video created from the broadcast. In the **Start** box, set the time when your broadcast should begin. In the **Audience** box, add people you would like to explicitly invite.

❺ Click **Share**.

❻ Once the Hangout has started, click **Start** from the automatically created Event page to which you are directed. This will broadcast the Hangout on Google+ and YouTube.

❼ Click on **Start Broadcast** once the Hangout has begun. This will change your Hangout from **Off Air** to **Live**.

❽ When finished, click **End Broadcast**. Your Hangout will continue until you close the Hangout window or click on the red phone at the top of your screen.

❾ Your Hangout on air archive will appear in your YouTube Video Manager.

How to
Share a YouTube Video
Within a Google+ Hangout

❶ Sign into your Google account. Go to the *Google+* website.
https://plus.google.com

❷ Click on **Start a video Hangout** in the lower right-hand corner.

❸ Send an invite. Do this by adding participants, circles, or email addresses you would like to join the Hangout. You can also include messages to invitees for easy identification.

❹ Click **Invite**.

❺ Fly your mouse over the left-hand side of the Hangout screen. You will see a variety of apps to add into your Hangout. Every person's list of apps is different, depending on how experienced you are at using Hangouts. However, everyone will see a YouTube logo and app. Click on **YouTube**.

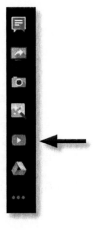

❻ Click **Add videos to playlist**.

© *Shell Education*   *#51312—Creating a Google Apps™ Classroom*

How to
Share a YouTube Video
Within a Google+ Hangout (cont.)

❼ Search for the video(s) you wish to share in your Hangout.

❽ Click the green plus button to add a video to the playlist.

❾ The video will automatically start. Click the pause button (**II**) to keep the video from automatically continuing.

❿ If you are sharing this video with others, ask them to click **YouTube** in the bar along the left-hand side of the Hangout to view the video(s) you have selected.

How to
Screen Share in a Google+ Hangout

❶ Sign into your Google account. Go to the *Google+* website.
https://plus.google.com

❷ Click on **Start a video Hangout** in the lower right-hand corner.

❸ Send an invite. Do this by adding participants, circles, or email addresses you would like to join the Hangout. You can also include messages to invitees for easy identification.

❹ Click **Invite**.

❺ Fly your mouse over the left-hand side of the Hangout screen. You will see a variety of apps to add into your Hangout. Every person's list of apps is different, depending on how experienced you are using Hangouts. However, everyone will see a screenshare icon and the word **Screenshare** will pop up if you fly your mouse over the icon. Click on the **Screenshare** icon.

❻ You will be given options for what, precisely, you want to share, including whether you want to share your desktop, the Google+ Hangout, or other possible options. Click on your choice.

❼ Click **Start Screenshare**.

❽ If, at any point, you want to cease the screensharing, click the **Screenshare** icon again. You can restart your screensharing anytime during the Google+ Hangout.

113

How to
Create a Google Voice Number

❶ Sign into your Google account. Go to the *Google Voice* website.
https://www.google.com/voice

❷ If you have never created a Google Voice number, you will be taken through a series of prompts—these are important to read before making your selections.

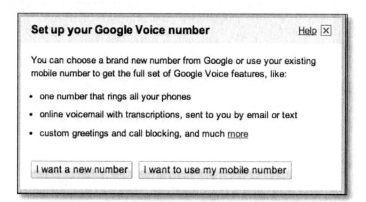

❸ Select **I want a new number** from the pop-up box in order to create a Google Voice number that is different from your personal phone number.

❹ At the next pop-up box, enter the home or mobile number that you want to ring when your Google Voice number is called. You can stop call forwarding to your personal number later by unchecking the box in the Google Voice settings.

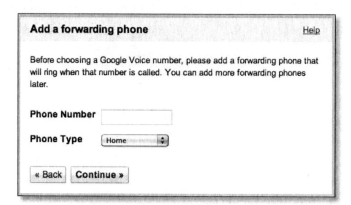

❺ Google will ask you to verify your phone number by entering a verification code from your phone. Google will call your phone when you click **Call me now**.

❻ Once you enter the verification code, your number will be verified and activated.

How to
Create a Google Voice Number *(cont.)*

❼ When selecting your new Google Voice number, you can enter the zip code or location of the area code you desire. You can also enter a set of numbers you would like in your number or a word you would like the numbers to spell out. It will try to generate a number that meets these requests.

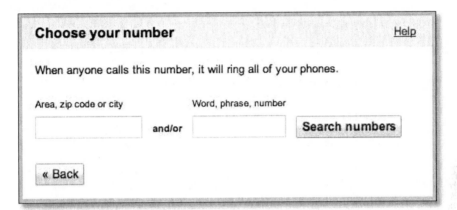

❽ Once you have found a number you like, select it by clicking the round button next to the number.

❾ Click **Continue**. Take note of your number and click **Finish**.

❿ To change the settings regarding how calls are forwarded to you, how voicemails are recorded or transcribed, who can call you, and more, click on the gear icon on the main voice page and select **Settings**. Here you can also record a voicemail greeting and select a voicemail PIN that will allow you to access your voicemail by phone.

#51312—*Creating a Google Apps™ Classroom*

How to
Create a Google Books Library

❶ Sign into your Google account. Go to the *Google Books* website. **https://books.google.com**

❷ Click on **My library** at the bottom of the page.

❸ In the search box at the top of the page, type the title of your favorite book, or a book to use with students.

❹ Click on the link to the title of the book that you choose.

❺ Click on the gray box at the top of the page that says **Add to my library**.

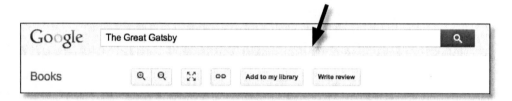

❻ There will be a drop-down menu from which you can choose which virtual bookshelf or bookshelves your chosen book will go into.

❼ Search again for a new book, and repeat instructions 5 and 6 for each book.

❽ When you are done, click on **My library** in the left-hand column to see your books organized into their digital bookshelves.

How to
Create a Google Books Bookshelf

❶ Sign into your Google account. Go to the *Google Books* website. **https://books.google.com**

❷ Click on **My Library** at the bottom of the page.

❸ Click on the red **New Shelf** button in the left-hand column.

❹ Name and describe your bookshelf here (i.e., Independent Reading, English 9, Science) and click **Create bookshelf**.

❺ In the search box at the top of the page, type the title of a book you wish to add to this bookshelf.

❻ Click on the link to the title of the book that you choose.

❼ Click on the gray box at the top of the page that says **Add to my library.**

❽ There will be a drop-down menu from which you can choose your new custom bookshelf.

❾ Return to your library once you are done, and you will see your new bookshelf listed in the left-hand column.

❿ Click on your **bookshelf**.

⓫ From here, you can make many more granular edits, as shown below, via the gear drop-down menu.

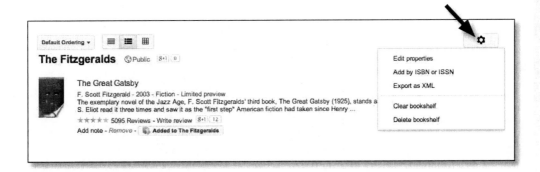

How to
Shorten a URL Using the Google URL Shortener

❶ Sign into your Google account. Go to the *Google URL Shortener* website. **https://goo.gl**

❷ Copy the URL from the site you are looking to shorten. The URL is the address that navigates to the site.

❸ Paste the URL into the box where it states **Paste your long URL here**.

❹ Click **Shorten URL**.

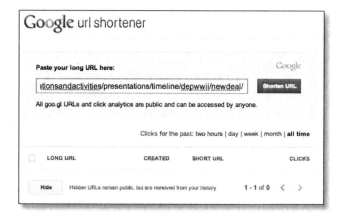

❺ Your shortened URL will appear in the same row as the original URL, under the column heading **SHORT URL**.

❻ You can copy this shortened URL to more easily share a link with others.

❼ Clicking **Details** next to the shortened URL will provide details for those who have accessed your shortened URL.

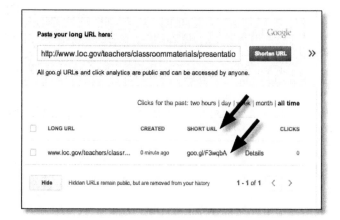

How to

Resize a QR Code from the Google URL Shortener

❶ Sign into your Google account. Go to the *Google URL Shortener* website. **https://goo.gl**

❷ Select a URL that you have previously shortened and click **Details** next to the shortened URL.

❸ The QR code can be found on the upper right-hand side of the page.

❹ Click on the QR code. The QR code will open in its own page.

❺ The URL for the QR code will appear at the top of the page. It will look similar to this URL.

← → C ◻ chart.googleapis.com/chart?cht=qr&chs=150x150&choe=UTF-8&chld=H&chl=http://goo.gl/F3wqbA

❻ The size of the image is found in the part of the URL in the format "chs=<width>x<height>."

❼ To resize the QR code, change the number of pixels listed in the "chs=" part of the URL without changing the rest of the URL.

❽ To make the QR code smaller, make the numbers smaller in the URL. To make the QR code larger, increase the size of numbers in the URL.

❾ The minimum size the QR code can be is 37 pixels by 37 pixels (chs=37x37).

❿ The maximum size the QR code can be is 547 pixels by 547 pixels (chs=547x547).

⓫ Once the QR code is the size you want, you can print it or copy the image and paste it wherever desired.

How to

Create an Account with an RSS Widget Creator that Will Create an "iFrame" Tag to Embed RSS Feeds

❶ Go to your choice of RSS Widget Creators. There are many options. These directions will use the RSSinclude.com website.
http://www.rssinclude.com

❷ Create a free account by using your Google Mail address.

❸ Click on **Start: Create a New RSS Feed Widget**.

❹ Use **Simple Vertical List** for most situations where the feed is a blog or other regularly published content. Click on the **Create Now** hyperlink.

❺ In the new window, on the **Input Feeds** tab, paste the URL for the feed that will be displayed in the widget. Click **Add Feed**.

❻ The **Content and Styling Options** tab will allow you to adjust the size and colors used in the widget.

❼ The **Get Include Snippet** tab provides several options for the type of code the widget will create. All Google applications prefer an iFrame tag over other tag formats. Click on the **iFrame** radio button to create the iFrame tag for the widget.

❽ Copy the code created in the **Your Code** box.

❾ Paste the code into any window where a Google application allows the editing of the HTML code.

❿ Save the document or site where the code was pasted.

⓫ Reload the page to see the content from the feed displayed in the current page.

How to
Create a Google Calendar

❶ Sign into your Google account. Go to the *Google Calendar* website. **https://calendar.google.com**

❷ Click on the small arrow to the right of the **My calendars** list along the left-hand side of the screen.

❸ Select **Create new calendar**.

❹ Name and describe the new calendar. Set your location and time zone.

 • **Note:** If you are going to post this calendar on a public website, make sure you click the **Make this calendar public** check box. You may also choose to share the calendar with specific people.

❺ Click **Create Calendar**.

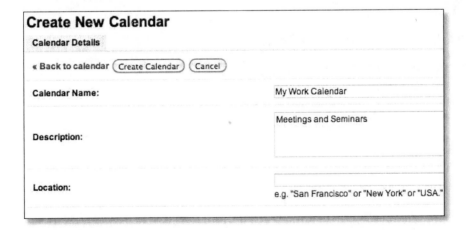

❻ To add an event to your calendar, navigate to the date and time of the event and click on that spot on the calendar. Enter the name of the event and check **Create Event** to add it to the calendar.

How to
Create a Blogger Page

❶ Sign into your Google account. Go to the *Blogger* website.
   https://www.blogger.com

❷ Click on the **New Blog** button.

❸ Title your blog, and give your blog a URL address (tip: use something easy
   to remember).

❹ Choose the template you would like to use for the blog and click
   Create blog!

How to
Create Filters in Gmail

❶ Sign into your Google account. Go to the *Google Mail* website.
https://mail.google.com/

❷ Click on the **gear** icon in the upper right-hand corner of your screen.

❸ Select **Settings**.

❹ Click the **Filters** tab across the top.

❺ Click the **Create a new filter** link.

❻ Complete the blank entry fields to your preferences.

❼ When the filter is to your specification, test the filter by clicking the blue **Spyglass** button at the bottom of the box. This will take you to all of the emails you currently have that fit your criteria.

❽ To return to the filter-creation page, you can click on the drop-down arrow at the end of the search box.

❾ You will be asked where or how you wish these emails to be handled in the future. If you want existing emails to be included, click the check box **Also apply filter to ___ matching conversations**.

❿ Once you are certain that your filter is how you want it to be, click **Create filter**.

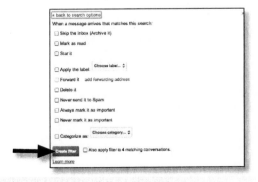

123

How to
Add a Gadget on a Blogger Page

❶ Sign into your Google account. Go to the *Blogger* website.
https://www.blogger.com

❷ Find the blog to which you would like to add a gadget.

❸ Next to the name of that blog, click on the drop-down menu next to the piece
of paper icon.

❹ Select **Layout**.

❺ Click on the space that indicates **Add a Gadget**.

❻ Browse for the gadget you would like, or click on **More Gadgets** to search for
a specific gadget.

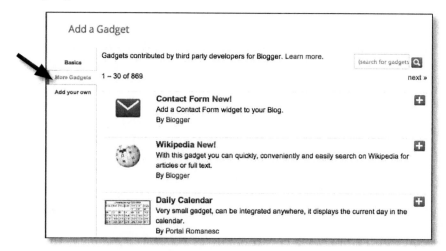

❼ Make sure to click **Preview** to view your changes and the new gadget before
clicking **Save arrangement**.

How to
Create a Recipe in IFTTT

❶ Go to the *IFTTT* website.
https://www.ifttt.com

❷ Create a free account in order to save your recipes and edit them later (if you so choose).

❸ Click on the blue **Use** botton.

Welcome to IFTTT

Recipes are simple connections that make your life easier.
Here's one to get you started.

Use

Every day, get a new recommended Recipe in your inbox

by kyle   2,405 uses

❹ Follow the on-screen instructions to create a recipe to streamline your workflow.

- **Note:** It can take up to 48 hours for your recipe to start working.

Notes

Notes

Notes